A
COVNTER-BLASTE

TO

TOBACCO

and

Other Intemperate
Diatribes against Tobacco

from the

Early Modern Period

London
Spradabach Publishing
2023

Spradabach Publishing
BM Box Spradabach
London WC1N 3XX

A Counterblaste to Tobacco and Other Intemperate Diatribes
against Tobacco from the Early Modern Period

First Spradabach edition published 2023
© Spradabach Publishing 2023

Interior design by Alex Kurtagic

ISBN 978-1-909606-35-7

British Library Cataloguing-in-Publication Data:
A catalogue record for this book is available from the British Library.

Table of Contents

Note on This Edition
vii

COVNTERBLASTE TO TOBACCO
1

Preface to the Reader
3

Covnterblaste to Tobacco
7

A Law of James against Tobacco
27

VVORK FOR CHIMNEY-SWEEPERS
31

To the Reader
33

Poem
37

Eight Reasons and Arguments
against Tobacco
41

A Warning to Tobacconists
43

THE WOMEN'S COMPLAINT
AGAINST TOBACCO
85

Index
99

Note on This Edition

he texts reproduced in this collection are all sourced from their respective first editions.

The spelling and punctuation in all cases remains as in the original, including the archaic use of u for v and v for u, but (1) ellided consonants indicated with a macron above the preceding vowel have been inserted and the macron removed; (2) the eszett has been rendered as a double 's'; and (3) punctuation has been added in a few, select passages where it appeard to be missing and it made logical sense.

A few obvious typographical errors have been silently corrected.

Editorial footnotes have been added and indentified accordingly.

An index has been generated.

A
Covnterblaste
to Tobacco

by

King James I

(1604)

Preface to the Reader

As every humane body (deare Countrey men) how wholesome soever, is notwithstanding subject, or at least naturally inclined to some sorts of diseases, or infirmities: so is there no Common-wealth, or Body-politicke, how well governed, or peaceable soever it bee, that lackes the owne popular errors, and naturally enclined corruptions: and therefore is it no wonder, although this our Countrey and Common-wealth, though peaceable, though wealthy, though long flourishing in both, be amongst the rest, subject to the owne naturall infirmities. We are of all Nations the people most loving and most reverently

3

obedient to our Prince, yet are wee (as time hath often borne witnesse) too easie to be seduced to make Rebellion, upon very slight grounds. Our fortunate and oft prooved valour in warres abroad, our heartie and reverent obedience to our Princes at home, hath bred us a long, and a thrice happy peace: Our Peace hath bred wealth: And Peace and wealth hath brought foorth a generall sluggishnesse, which makes us wallow in all sorts of idle delights, and soft delicacies, the first seedes of the subversion of all great Monarchies. Our Cleargie are become negligent and lazie, our Nobilitie and Gentrie prodigall, and solde to their private delights, Our Lawyers covetous, our Commonpeople prodigall and curious; and generally all sorts of people more carefull for their privat ends, then for their mother the Common-wealth.

For remedie whereof, it is the Kings part (as the proper Phisician of his Politicke-body) to purge it of all those diseases, by Medicines meete for the same: as by a certaine milde, and yet just forme of government, to maintain the publicke quietnesse, and prevent all occasions of Commotion: by the example of his owne Person and Court, to make us all ashamed of our sluggish delicacie, and to stirre us up to the practise againe of all honest exercises, and Martiall shadowes of Warre; As likewise by his, and his Courts moderatenesse in Apparell, to make us ashamed of our prodigalitie. By his quicke admonitions and careful overseeing of the Cleargie, to waken them up againe, to be more diligent

4

in their Offices: By the sharpe triall, and severe punishment of the partiall, covetous and bribing Lawyers, to reforme their corruptions: And generally by the example of his owne Person, and by the due execution of good Lawes, to reforme and abolish, piece and piece, these old and evill grounded abuses. For this will not bee *Opus unius diei*,[1] but as every one of these diseases, must from the King receive the owne cure proper for it, so are there some sorts of abuses in Commonwealths, that though they be of so base and contemptible a condition, as they are too low for the Law to looke on, and too meane for a King to interpone his anthoritie, or bend his eye upon: yet are they corruptions, as well as the greatest of them. So is an Ant an Animal, aswell as an Elephant: so is a Wrenne Avis, aswell as a Swanne, and so is a small dint of the Toothake, a disease aswell as the fearefull Plague is. But for these base sorts of corruption in Common-wealthes, not onely the King, or any inferior Magistrate, but *Quilibet e populo*[2] may serve to be a Phisician, by discovering and impugning the error, and by perswading reformation thereof.

And surely in my opinion, there cannot be a more base, and yet hurtfull, corruption in a Countrey, then is the vile use (or other abuse) of taking Tobacco in this Kingdome, which hath moved me, shortly to discover the abuses thereof in this following little Pamphlet.

---

1   'A work of one day only'. —Ed.

2   'Whoever of the people may please'. —Ed.

If any thinke it a light Argument, so is it but a toy that is bestowed upon it. And since the Subject is but of Smoke, I thinke the fume of an idle braine, may serve for a sufficient battery against so fumous and feeble an enemy. If my grounds be found true, it is all I looke for; but if they cary the force of perswasion with them, it is all, I can wish and more then I can expect. My onely care is, that you, my deare Countrey-men, may rightly conceive even by this smallest trifle, of the sinceritie of my meaning in greater matters, never to spare any paine, that may tend to the procuring of your weale and prosperitie.

Covnterblaste to Tobacco

That the manifolde abuses of this vile custome of Tobacco taking, may the better be espied, it is fit, that first you enter into consideration both of the first originall thereof, and likewise of the reasons of the first entry thereof into this Countrey. For certainely as such customes, that have their first institution either from a godly, necessary, or honorable ground, and are first brought in, by the meanes of some worthy, vertuous, and great Personage, are ever, and most justly, holden in great and reverent estimation and account, by all wise, vertuous, and temperate spirits: So should it by the contrary, justly bring a great disgrace into that sort of customes, which having their originall from base corruption and barbarity, doe in like sort, make their first entry into a Countrey, by an inconsiderate and childish affectation of Noveltie, as is the true case of the first invention of Tobacco taking, and of the first entry thereof among us. For Tobacco being a common herbe, which (though under divers names) growes almost every where, was first found out by some of the barbarous Indians, to be a Preservative, or Antidot against the Pockes, a filthy disease, whereunto these barbarous people are (as all men know) very much subject, what through the uncleanly and adust constitution of their bodies, and what through the intemperate heate of their Climat: so that as from them was first brought into Christendome, that most detestable disease, so from them likewise was brought this use of Tobacco, as a stinking and unsavorie Antidot, for so corrupted and execrable a Maladie, the stinking Suffumigation whereof they yet use against that disease, making so one canker or venime to eate out another.

And now good Countrey men let us (I pray you) consider, what honour or policie can moove us to imitate the barbarous and beastly maners of the wilde, godlesse, and slavish Indians, especially in so vile and stinking a custome? Shall wee that disdaine to imitate the maners of our neighbour France (having the stile of the first Christian Kingdom) and that cannot endure the spirit of the Spaniards (their King being now comparable in

largenes of Dominions, to the great Emperor of
Turkie); shall wee, I say, that have bene so long
civill and wealthy in Peace, famous and invinci-
ble in Warre, fortunate in both, we that have bene
ever able to aide any of our neighbours (but never
deafed any of their eares with any of our supplica-
tions for assistance); shall we, I say, without blush-
ing, abase our selves so farre, as to imitate these
beastly Indians, slaves to the Spaniards, refuse to
the world, and as yet aliens from the holy Cove-
nant of God? Why doe we not as well imitate them
in walking naked as they doe? in preferring glass-
es, feathers, and such toyes, to golde and precious
stones, as they do? yea why do we not denie God
and adore the Devill, as they doe?

Now to the corrupted basenesse of the first use
of this Tobacco, doeth very well agree the foolish
and groundlesse first entry thereof into this Kingdome. It is not so long since the first entry of this
abuse amongst us here, as this present age cannot
yet very well remember, both the first Author, and
the forme of the first introduction of it amongst us.
It was neither brought in by King, great Conquero-
ur, nor learned Doctor of Phisicke.

With the report of a great discovery for a Con-
quest, some two or three Savage men, were brought
in, together with this Savage custome. But the pitie is, the poore wilde barbarous men died, but that
vile barbarous custome is yet alive, yea in fresh vig-
or: so as it seemes a miracle to me, how a custome
springing from so vile a ground, and brought in by a

father so generally hated, should be welcomed upon so slender a warrant. For if they that first put it in practise heere, had remembred for what respect it was used by them from whence it came, I am sure they would have bene loath, to have taken so farre the imputation of that disease upon them as they did, by using the cure thereof. For *Sanis non est opus medico,*[1] and counterpoisons are never used, but where poyson is thought to precede.

But since it is true, that divers customes slightly grounded, and with no better warrant entred in a Commonwealth, may yet in the use of them thereafter, proove both necessary and profitable; it is therefore next to be examined, if there be not a full Sympathie and true Proportion, betweene the base ground and foolish entrie, and the loathsome, and hurtfull use of this stinking Antidote.

I am now therefore heartily to pray you to consider, first upon what false and erroneous grounds you have first built the generall good liking thereof; and next, what sinnes towards God, and foolish vanities before the world you commit, in the detestable use of it.

As for these deceitfull grounds, that have specially mooved you to take a good and great conceit thereof, I shall content my selfe to examine here onely foure of the principals of them; two founded upon the Theoricke of a deceivable appearance of Reason, and two of them upon the mistaken Practicke of generall Experience.

---

1   'The healthy person is not the concern of the doctor'. —Ed.

First, it is thought by you a sure Aphorisme in the Physickes, That the braines of all men, beeing naturally colde and wet, all dry and hote things should be good for them; of which nature this stinking suffumigation is, and therefore of good use to them. Of this Argument, both the Proposition and Assumption are false, and so the Conclusion cannot but be voyd of it selfe. For as to the Proposition, That because the braines are colde and moist, therefore things that are hote and drie are best for them, it is an inept consequence: For man beeing compounded of the foure Complexions, (whose fathers are the foure Elements) although there be a mixture of them all in all the parts of his body, yet must the divers parts of our Microcosme or little world within our selves, be diversly more inclined, some to one, some to another complexion, according to the diversitie of their uses, that of these discords a perfect harmonie may bee made up for the maintenance of the whole body.

The application then of a thing of a contrary nature, to any of these parts, is to interrupt them of their due function, and by consequence hurtfull to the health of the whole body. As if a man, because the Liver is hote (as the fountaine of blood) and as it were an oven to the stomacke, would therfore apply and weare close upon his Liver and stomacke a cake of lead; he might within a very short time (I hope) be susteined very good cheape at an Ordinarie, beside the cleering of his conscience from that deadly sinne of gluttonie.

And as if, because the Heart is full of vitall spirits, and in perpetuall motion, a man would therefore lay a heavy pound stone on his breast, for staying and holding downe that wanton palpitation, I doubt not but his breast would bee more bruised with the weight thereof, then the heart would be comforted with such a disagreeable and contrarious cure. And even so is it with the Braines. For if a man, because the Braines are colde and humide, would therefore use inwardly by smells, or outwardly by application, things of hot and drie qualitie, all the gaine that he could make thereof, would onely be to put himselfe in a great forwardnesse for running mad, by over-watching him selfe, the coldnesse and moistnesse of is our braine beeing the onely ordinarie meanes that procure our sleepe and rest. Indeed I do not denie, but when it falls out that any of these, or any part of our bodie growes to be distempered, and to tend to ail extremitie, beyond the compasse of Natures temperate mixture, that in that case cures of contrary qualities, to the intemperate inclination of that part, being wisely prepared and discreetely ministered, may be both necessarie and helpfull for strengthning and assisting Nature in the expulsion of her enemies: for this is the true definition of all profitable Physicke.

But first these Cures ought not to bee used, but where there is neede of them, the contrarie whereof, is daily practised in this generall use of Tobacco by all sorts and complexions of people.

And next, I deny the Minor of this argument, as I have already said, in regard that this Tobacco, is not simply of a dry and hot qualitie; but rather hath a certaine venemous facultie joyned with the heate thereof, which makes it have an Antipathie against nature, as by the hatefull smell thereof doeth well appeare. For the Nose being the proper Organ and convoy of the sense of smelling to the braines, which are the onely fountaine of that sense, doeth ever serve us for an infallible witnesse, whether that Odour which we smell, be healthfull or hurtfull to the braine (except when it fals out that the sense it selfe is corrupted and abused through some infirmitie, and distemper in the braine.) And that the suffumigation thereof cannot have a drying qualitie, it needes no further probation, then that it is a smoake, all smoake and vapour, being of it selfe humide, as drawing neere to the nature of the ayre, and easie to be resolved againe into water, whereof there needes no other proofe but the Meteors, which being bred of nothing else but of the vapours and exhalations sucked up by the Sunne out of the earth, the Sea, and waters yet are the same smoakie vapours turned, and transformed into Raynes, Snowes, Deawes, hoare Frostes, and such like waterie Meteors, as by the contrarie the raynie cloudes are often transformed and evaporated in blustering winds.

The second Argument grounded on a show of reason is, That this filthie smoake, as well through the heat and strength thereof, as by a naturall force and qualitie, is able and fit to purge both the head and stomacke of Rhewmes and distillations, as experience teacheth, by the spitting and avoyding fleame, immediately after the taking of it. But the fallacie of this Argument may easily appeare, by my late preceding description of the Meteors. For even as the smoakie vapours sucked up by the Sunne, and staied in the lowest and colde Region of the ayre, are there contracted into cloudes and turned into raine and such other watery Meteors: So this stinking smoake being sucked up by the Nose, and imprisoned in the colde and moyst braines, is by their colde and wett facultie, turned and cast foorth againe in waterie distillations, and so are you made free and purged of nothing, but that wherewith you wilfully burdened your selves: and therefore are you no wiser in taking Tobacco for purging you of distillations, then if for preventing the Cholike you would take all kinde of windie meates and drinkes, and for preventing of the Stone, you would take all kinde of meates and drinkes that would breede gravell in the Kidneyes, and then when you were forced to avoyde much winde out of your stomacke, and much gravell in your Urine, that you should attribute the thanke thereof to such nourishments as bred those within you, that behoved either to be expelled by the force of Nature, or you to have burst at the broadside, as the Proverbe is.

As for the other two reasons founded upon experience, the first of which is, That the whole people would not have taken so generall a good liking thereof, if they had not by experience found it verie soveraigne and good for them: For answere thereunto how easily the mindes of any people, wherewith God hath replenished this world, may be drawn to the foolish affectation of any noveltie, I leave it to the discreet judgement of any man that is reasonable.

Doe we not dayly see, that a man can no sooner bring over from beyond the Seas any new forme of apparell, but that hee can not bee thought a man of spirit, that would not presently imitate the same? And so from hand to hand it spreades, till it be practised by all, not for any commoditie that is in it, but only because it is come to be the fashion. For such is the force of that naturall Selfe-love in every one of us, and such is the corruption of envie bred in the brest of every one, as we cannot be content unlesse we imitate every thing that our fellowes doe, and so proove our selves capable of every thing whereof they are capable, like Apes, counterfeiting the maners of others, to our owne destruction. For let one or two of the greatest Masters of Mathematickes in any of the two famous Universities, but constantly affirme any cleare day, that they see some strange apparition in the skies: they will I warrant you be seconded by the greatest part of the Students in that profession: So loath will they be, to bee thought inferiour to their fellowes, either in depth of knowledge or sharpnesse of sight: And therefore the generall good liking and imbracing of this foolish custome, doeth but onely proceede from that affectation of noveltie, and popular errour, whereof I have already spoken.

The other argument drawen from a mistaken experience, is but the more particular probation of this generall, because it is alleaged to be found true by proofe, that by the taking of Tobacco divers and very many doe finde themselves cured of divers diseases as on the other part, no man ever received harme thereby. In this argument there is first a great mistaking and next a monstrous absurditie. For is it not a very great mistaking, to take *Non causam pro causa*,[2] as they say in the Logicks? because peradventure when a sicke man hath had his disease at the height, hee hath at that instant taken Tobacco, and afterward his disease taking the naturall course of declining, and consequently the patient of recovering his health, O then the Tobacco forsooth, was the worker of that miracle. Beside that, it is a thing well knowen to all Phisicians, that the apprehension and conceit of the patient hath by wakening and uniting the vitall spirits, and so strengthening nature, a great power and vertue, to cure divers diseases. For an evident proofe of mistaking in the like case, I pray you what foolish boy, what sillie wench, what olde doting wife, or ignorant countrey clowne, is not a Phisician for the toothach, for the cholicke, and divers such common diseases? Yea, will not every man you meete withal, teach you a sundry cure for

---

2   'Confusing something that is not the cause, for the cause'. —Ed.

the same, and sweare by that meane either himselfe, or some of his neerest kinsmen and friends was cured? And yet I hope no man is so foolish as to beleeve them. And al these toyes do only proceed from the mistaking *Non causam pro causa*, as I have already sayd, and so if a man chance to recover one of any disease, after he hath taken Tobacco, that must have the thankes of all. But by the contrary, if a man smoke himselfe to death with it (and many have done) O then some other disease must beare the blame for that fault. So doe olde harlots thanke their harlotrie for their many yeeres, that custome being healthfull (say they) *ad purgandos Renes*,[3] but never have minde how many die of the Pockes in the flower of their youth. And so doe olde drunkards thinke they prolong their dayes, by their swinelike diet, but never remember howe many die drowned in drinke before they be halfe olde.

And what greater absurditie can there bee, then to say that one cure shall serve for divers, nay, contrarious sortes of diseases? It is all undoubted ground among all Phisicians, that there is almost no sort either of nourishment or medicine, that hath not some thing in it disagreeable to some part of mans bodie, because, as I have already sayd, the nature of the temperature of every part, is so different from another, that according to the olde proverbe, That which is good for the head, is evill for the necke and the shoulders. For

---

3   'For purifying the loins'. —Ed.

even as a strong enemie, that invades a towne or fortresse, although in his siege thereof, he do belaie and compasse it round about, yet he makes his breach and entrie, at some one or few special parts thereof, which hee hath tried and found to bee weakest and least able to resist; so sickenesse doth make her particular assault, upon such part or parts of our bodie, as are weakest and easiest to be overcome by that sort of disease, which then doth assaile us, although all the rest of the body by Sympathie feele it selfe, to be as it were belaied, and besieged by the affliction of that speciall part, the griefe and smart thereof being by the sence of feeling dispersed through all the rest of our members. And therefore the skilfull Phisician presses by such cures, to purge and strengthen that part which is afflicted, as are only fit for that sort of disease, and doe best agree with the nature of that infirme part; which being abused to a disease of another nature, would proove as hurtfull for the one, as helpfull for the other. Yea, not only will a skilfull and warie Phisician bee carefull to use no cure but that which is fit for that sort of disease, but he wil also consider all other circumstances, and make the remedies sutable thereunto: as the temperature of the clime where the Patient is, the constitution of the Planets, the time of the Moone, the season of the yere, the age and complexion of the Patient, and the present state of his body, in strength or weaknesse. For one cure must not ever be used for the self-same disease, but according to the varying of any of the foresaid circumstances, that sort of remedie must be used which is fittest for the same. Whear by the contrarie in this case, such is the miraculous omnipotencie of our strong tasted Tobacco, as it cures all sorts of diseases (which never any drugge could do before) in all persons, and at all times. It cures all manner of distillations, either in the head or stomacke (if you beleeve their Axiomes) although in very deede it doe both corrupt the braine, and by causing over quicke digestion, fill the stomacke full of crudities. It cures the Gowt in the feet, and (which is miraculous) in that very instant when the smoke thereof, as light, flies up into the head, the vertue thereof, as heavie, runs downe to the little toe. It helpes all sorts of Agues. It makes a man sober that was drunke. It refreshes a weary man, and yet makes a man hungry. Being taken when they goe to bed, it makes one sleepe soundly, and yet being taken when a man is sleepie and drowsie, it will, as they say, awake his braine, and quicken his understanding. As for curing of the Pockes, it serves for that use but among the pockie Indian slaves. Here in England it is refined, and will not deigne to cure heere any other then cleanly and gentlemanly diseases. O omnipotent power of Tobacco! And if it could by the smoke thereof chace out devils, as the smoke of Tobias fish did (which I am sure could smel no stronglier) it would serve for a precious Relicke, both for the superstitious Priests, and the insolent Puritanes, to cast out devils withall.

Admitting then, and not confessing that the use thereof were healthfull for some sortes of diseases; should it be used for all sicknesses? should it be used by all men? should it be used at al times? yea should it be used by able, yong, strong, healthful men? Medicine hath that vertue, that it never leaveth a man in that state wherin it findeth him: it makes a sicke man whole, but a whole man sicke. And as Medicine helpes nature being taken at times of necessitie, so being ever and continually used, it doth but weaken, wearie, and weare nature. What speake I of Medicine? Nay let a man every houre of the day, or as oft as many in this countrey use to take Tobacco, let a man I say, but take as oft the best sorts of nourishments in meate and drinke that can bee devised, hee shall with the continuall use thereof weaken both his head and his stomacke: all his members shall become feeble, his spirits dull, and in the end, as a drowsie lazie belly-god, he shall evanish in a Lethargie.

And from this weaknesse it proceeds, that many in this kingdome have had such a continuall use of taking this uusavorie smoke, as now they are not able to forbeare the same, no more then an olde drunkard can abide to be long sober, without falling into an uncurable weaknesse and evill constitution: for their continuall custome hath made to them, *habitum, alteram naturam:*[4] so to those that from their birth have bene continually nour-

----
4   'Habit is second nature'. —Ed.

ished upon poison and things venemous, wholesome meates are onely poisonable.

Thus having, as I truste, sufficiently answered
the most principall arguments that are used in
defence of this vile custome, it rests onely to informe you what sinnes and vanities you commit in
the filthie abuse thereof. First, are you not guiltie
of sinnefull and shamefull lust? (for lust may bee
as well in any of the senses as in feeling) that although you bee troubled with no disease, but in
perfect health, yet can you neither be merry at an
Ordinarie, nor lascivious in the Stewes, if you lacke
Tobacco to provoke your appetite to any of those
sorts of recreation, lusting after it as the children
of Israel did in the wildernesse after Quailes? Secondly it is, as you use or rather abuse it, a branche
of the sinne of drunkennesse, which is the roote
of all sinnes: for as the onely delight that drunkards take in Wine is in the strength of the taste,
and the force of the fume thereof that mounts up
to the braine: for no drunkards love any weake,
or sweete drinke: so are not those (I meane the
strong heate and the fume) the onely qualities that
make Tobacco so delectable to all the lovers of
it? And as no man likes strong headie drinke the
first day (because *nemo repente fit turpissimus*)[5]
but by custome is piece and piece allured, while in
the ende, a drunkard will have as great a thirst to
bee drunke, as a sober man to quench his thirst
with a draught when hee hath need of it: So is not

---

5   'No man ever became extremely wicked all at once'. —Ed.

this the very case of all the great takers of Tobacco? which therefore they themselves do attribute to a bewitching qualitie in it. Thirdly, is it not the greatest sinne of all, that you the people of all sortes of this Kingdome, who are created and ordeined by God to bestowe both your persons and goods for the maintenance both of the honour and safetie of your King and Commonweath, should disable your selves in both? In your persons having by this continuall vile custome brought your selves to this shameful imbecilitie, that you are not able to ride or walke the journey of a Jewes Sabboth, but you must have a reekie cole brought you from the next Poore house to kindle your Tobacco with? whereas he cannot be thought able for any service in the warres, that cannot endure oftentimes the want of meate, drinke and sleepe, much more then must hee endure the want of Tobacco. In the times of the many glorious and victorious battailes fought by this Nation, there was no word of Tobacco. But now if it were time of warres, and that you were to make some sudden Cavalcado upon your enemies, if any of you should seeke leisure to stay behinde his fellowe for taking of Tobacco, for my part I should never bee sorie for any evill chance that might befall him. To take a custome in any thing that cannot bee left againe, is most harmefull to the people of any land. Mollicies and delicacie were the wracke and overthrow, first of the Persian, and next of the Romane Empire. And this very custome of taking Tobacco (whereof our present purpose is) is even at this day accounted so effeminate among the Indians themselves, as in the market they will offer no price for a slave to be sold, whome they finde to be a great Tobacco taker.

Now how you are by this custome disabled in your goods, let the Gentry of this land beare witnesse, some of them bestowing three, some foure hundred pounds a yeere upon this precious stinke, which I am sure might be bestowed upon many farre better uses. I read indeede of a knavish Courtier, who for abusing the favour of the Emperour Alexander Severus his Master by taking bribes to intercede, for sundry persons in his Masters eare (for whom he never once opened his mouth) was justly choked with smoke, with this doome, *Fumo pereat, qui fumum vendidit*:[6] but of so many smoke-buyers, as are at this present in this kingdome, I never read nor heard.

And for the vanities committed in this filthie custome, is it not both great vanitie and uncleanenesse, that at the table, a place of respect, of cleanlinesse, of modestie, men should not be ashamed, to sit tossing of Tobacco pipes, and puffing of the smoke of Tobacco one to another, making the filthy smoke and stinke thereof, to exhale athwart the dishes, and infect the aire, when very often, men that abhorre it are at their repast? Surely Smoke becomes a kitchin far better then a Dining chamber, and yet it makes a kitchin also oftentimes in the inward parts of men, soiling and infecting

6   'May he die from smoke, who sold smoke'. —Ed.

them, with an unctuous and oily kinde of Soote, as hath bene found in some great Tobacco takers, that after their death were opened. And not one-ly meate time, but no other time nor action is exempted from the publike use of this uncivill tricke: so as if the wives of Diepe list to contest with this Nation for good maners their worst maners would in all reason be found at least not so dishonest (as ours are) in this point. The publike use whereof, at all times, and in all places, hath now so farre prevailed, as divers men very sound both in judgement, and complexion, have bene at last forced to take it also without desire, partly because they were ashamed to seeme singular, (like the two Philosophers that were forced to duck themselves in that raine water, and so become fooles aswell as the rest of the people) and partly, to be as one that was content to eate Garlicke (which hee did not love) that he might not be troubled with the smell of it, in the breath of his fellowes. And is it not a great vanitie, that a man cannot heartily welcome his friend now, but straight they must bee in hand with Tobacco? No it is become in place of a cure, a point of good fellowship, and he that will refuse to take a pipe of Tobacco among his fellowes, (though by his own election he would rather feele the savour of a Sinke) is accounted peevish and no good company, even as they doe with tippeling in the cold Easterne Countries. Yea the Mistresse cannot in a more manerly kinde, entertaine her servant, then by giving him out of her faire hand a pipe of Tobacco. But herein is not onely a great vanitie but a great contempt of Gods good giftes, that the sweetenesse of mans breath, being a good gift of God, should be willfully corrupted by this stinking smoke, wherein I must confesse, it hath too strong a vertue: and so that which is an ornament of nature, and can neither by any artifice be at the first acquired, nor once lost, be recovered againe, shall be filthily corrupted with an incurable stinke, which vile qualitie is as directly contrary to that wrong opinion which is holden of the wholesomnesse thereof, as the venime of putrifaction is contrary to the vertue Preservative.

Moreover, which is a great iniquitie, and against all humanitie, the husband shall not bee ashamed, to reduce thereby his delicate, wholesome, and cleane complexioned wife, to that extremitie, that either shee must also corrupt her sweete breath therewith, or else resolve to live in a perpetuall stinking torment.

Have you not reason then to bee ashamed, and to forbeare this filthie noveltie, so basely grounded, so foolishly received and so grossely mistaken in the right use thereof? In your abuse thereof sinning against God, harming your selves both in persons and goods, and raking also thereby the markes and notes of vanitie upon you: by the custome thereof making your selves to be wondered at by all forraine civil Nations, and by all strangers that come among you, to be scorned and contemned. A custome lothsome to the eye, hatefull to the Nose, harmefull to the braine, dangerous to the Lungs, and in the blacke stinking fume thereof, neerest resembling the horrible Stigian smoke of the pit that is bottomelesse.

A Law of James against Tobacco

he foregoing Invective was written by the King of Great Britain. How early its royal authorship was avowed, I know not: but it was generally known long before its insertion in the collected edition of the King's Workes, published in 1616.[1]

King James stopped not, in his Crusade against Tobacco, at words. In the following *Commissio pro Tabacco* he added Fines and Blows:

JAMES, by the Grace of God &c. to our right

---

1   *Workes of the most high and mightie prince, James by the grace of God, King of Great Britaine, France and Ireland, defender of the faith, &c. Collection of His Maiesties workes* (London: James, Bishop of Winton, 1616). —Ed.

Trustie and right Welbeloved Cousen and Counsellor, Thomas Earle of Dorset our High Treasourer of Englande, Greetinge.

Whereas Tabacco being a Drugge of late Yeres found out, and by Merchants, as well Denizens as Strangers, brought from forreign Partes in small quantitie into this Realm of England and other our Dominions, was used and taken by the better sort both then and nowe onelye as Phisicke to preserve Healthe, and is now at this Day, through evell Custome and the Toleration thereof, excessivelie taken by a nomber of ryotous and disordered Persons of meane and base Condition, whoe, contrarie to the use which Persons of good Callinge and Qualitye make thereof, doe spend most of there tyme in that idle Vanitie, to the evill example and corrupting of others, and also do consume that Wages whiche manye of them gett by theire Labour, and wherewith there Families should be releived, not caring at what Price they buye that Drugge, but rather devisinge how to add to it other Mixture, therebye to make it the more delightfull to their Taste, though so much the more costly to there Purse; by which great and imoderate takinge of Tabacco the Health of a great nomber of our People is impayred, and theire Bodies weakened and made unfit for Labor, the Estates of many mean Persons soe decayed and consumed as they are thereby dryven to unthriftie Shifts onelie to maynteyne their gluttonous exercise thereof, besides that also a great part of the Treasure of our Lande is spent and exhausted by this onely Drugge so licentiously abused by the meaner sorte, all which enormous Inconveniences ensuinge thereuppon We doe well perceave to proceed principally from the great quantitie of Tabacco daily brought into this our Realm of England and Dominions of Wales from the Partes beyond the Seas by Merchauntes and others, which Excesse We conceave might in great part be restrayned by some good Imposition to be laid uppon it, whereby it is likelie that a lesse Quantitie of Tabacco will hereafter be broughte into this our Realm of Englaud, Dominion of Wales and Town of Barwick then in former tymes, and yet sufficient store to serve for their necessarie use who are of the better sort, and have and will use the same with Moderation to preserve their Healthe;

We do therefore will and command you our Treasurer of Englande, and herebye also warrant and aucthorise you to geve order to all Customers Comptrollers Searchers Surveyors, and all other Officers of our Portes, that, from and after the sixe and twentith Day of October next comynge, they shall demaunde and take to our use of all Merchauntes, as well Englishe as Strangers, and of all others whoe shall bringe in anye Tabacco into this Realme, within any Porte Haven or Creek belonging to any theire severall Charges, the Somme of Six Shillinges and eighte Pence uppon everye Pound Waight thereof, over and above the Custome of Twoo Pence uppon the Pounde Waighte usuallye paide heretofore;

And for the better execution hereof, bothe in the Reformation of the saide Abuses, and for the avoydinge of all Fraude and Deceipte concerninge the Paymente of the saide Imposition and Custome, Our Will and Pleasure is that you shall in our Name straightlye charge and commaunde all Collectors Customers Comptrollers Surveyors, and other Officers whatsoever to whome the same maye belonge, that they suffer noe Entries to be made of anye Tabacco at anye tyme hereafter to be broughte into anye Porte Haven or Creeke within this our Realme of Englande, the Dominion of Wales, and Towne of Barwicke, or anye parte of the same, by anye Englishe or Stranger, or anye other Persone whatsoever, before the saide Custome and Imposition before specified be firste satisfied and paide, or Composition made for the same with oure saide Customers, Collectors, or other Officers to whome the enme apperteyneth, uppon Payne that if anye Merchaunte Englishe or Straunger, or other whatsoever, shall presume to bringe in anye of the saide Tabacco, before suche Payemente and Satisfactione firste made, That then he shall not onelie forfeite the saide Tabacco, but alsoe shall undergoe suche furthere Penalties and corporall Punishmente as the Qualitie of suche soe highe a Coutempte against our Royall and expresse Commaundemente in this mannere published shall deserve.

Wytnes our self at Westminster the seaventeenth Day of October. [1604].

Per ipsum Regem.

Rymer Fœdera, xvi. 601. Ed. 1715.

VVork for Chimny-Sweepers:

or

A Warning for Tabacconists.

Describing the Pernicious vse of Tabacco,
no Lesse Pleasant then Profitable for
All Sorts to Reade

Fummus patria, igne alieno Luculentior

As much to say,

Better to be chokt with English hemp,
than be poisoned with Indian Tobacco.

by

Philaretes

(1602)

To the Reader

am to well asured (good Reader) that in vndertaking this vaine discourse of the pernicious & vulgar vse or rather abuse of Tabacco, I shall draw vnto my selfe no small hatred among our smoky gallants, who hauing long time glutted themselues with the fond fopperies and fashions of our neighbour Countries: yet still desirous of nouelties, haue not stucke to trauell as farre as India to fetch a *Dulce venenum*, a graecian Helen, an insatiate Messaline, and hugge a stinging serpent in their bosomes: nor am I ignorant, that to the wiser sort this treatise will seeme at the first a fruitlesse labour, of an idle braine, and to other some a vaine florish of a carping minde: And

that beecause in this treatise is vtterly reprehend-
ed and in some sort refuted, that which of many
excellent & learned men hath beene most highly
commended, and by sundry persons of high estate
hath beene experimented and tryed verie commo-
dious for the health of man.

For Monardus in his treatise of the West Indian simples,[1] Carolus Clusius in his *Comment vpon
Garcaeas de Stirpibus et Aromaticis Indicis*, and
Baptista Porta in his 8. booke and 11. Chap: of *Naturall Magick*[2] doe commend this plant as a thing
most excellent and diuine.

And in these our daies many excellent Phisitions and men of singuler learning and practise,
together with many gentlemen and some of great
accompt, doe by their daily vse and custome in
drinking of Tabacco, giue great credit and authoritie to the same: yet neuerthelesse if it shall
please them either with patience to heare, or with
iudgement to reade these few lines, and with in-
differencie to waie and ponder the reasons herein
aleadged, I doubt not but they shall finde, neither

---

1   Nicolás Monardes, *Segunda parte del libro des las cosas que
     se traen de nuestras Indias Occidentales, que sirven al uso de
     la medicina; do se trata del tabaco, y de la sassafras, y del
     carlo sancto, y de otras muchas yervas y plantas, simientes,
     y licores que agora nuevamente han venido de aqulellas
     partes, de grandes virtudes y maravillosos effectos* (Sevilla:
     Alonso Escrivano, 1571). —Ed.

2   Giambattista della Porta, *Natural Magick* (London: Thomas
     Young and Samuel Speed, 1658). Revised and expanded Latin
     original: *Magiæ Naturalis*, 20 vols. (Naples, 1589). —Ed.

the great authoritie of the one, nor the vsuall practise of the other, nor yet them both vnited and conioined in one, a ground for this their vulgar practise of a thing so hurtfull and pernitious to the life and health of man.

Authorities of expert and learned men in their art (I confesse) bee motiues of waight and importance to leade and draw the vnlearned and vnskilfull sort, who for the more part sticke and relie more on the authoritie of the teacher, then on his demonstrations and proofes, to yeeld to their assertions.

But of all heresies in Philosophie that Pithagoricall precept (*Ipse dixit*)[3] seemeth most grose, hurtfull, and pernitious: Heerevpon wee finde that *Aristotle* in his *Morals* thought it not a matter of wisedome or worth commendacion, to content himselfe with the bare authoritie of his Maister Plato (who no doubt was in learning most excellent: but laying Platoes assertions in one skale of the ballance, and reason with experience in the other, and finding his Maisters authoritie to light to counterpease reason, hee made it no scruple to swarue and discent from *Ipse dixit*, and stuck to sensible reason, as a most euident meanes to bring a sensible and reasonable creature, to the knowledge and vnderstanding of the truth.

The like in Phisicke did Galen, dissenting sometimes from his Master Hipocrates, (for so may I terme him, for from him he had his light:) & of

---

3   A dogmatic and unproven statement. —Ed.

set purpose in his Comments on Hippocrates Epidemicks, and Aphorismes doth refute him: And Aristotle had wont to say, *Amicus Plato, sed Magis amica veritas.* Plato was his friend, (for from him hee had his learning and knowledge) but Truth and Veritie was his greater friend, and therfore in equitie & right hee ought rather to take hir part.

So for truth sake onely did Varro write against Lelius, Sulpitius against Casselius, Saint Ierome against Hilaris, Saint Augustine against Hierome and Ambrose also. These men made euer more accompt and estimation of veritie and truth, then of the authoritie of learning in any whosoeuer.

Let it not therefore (good Reader) seeme a vaine thing to you, or an argument of an Idle braine, for mee to discent in iudgement of Tabacco, from those authors before aleaged, hauing as I suppose, both sollide Reasons and true Experience on my side to counterpease their authorities founded rather on opinion then any certaine science or demonstration.

Philaretes.

ot the desire of any priuate game,
Nor motions of a Carping braine,
Nor for reward from some *Mecænas* file,
(How euer men may Censure them life,)
Nor the desire to see my name in print,
Like pupill Poets whose mindes looke a squint,
To heart the Vulger sorts applauding voice,
Commend their budding Mule, Inuentions Choice:
    Hath forc't mee take in hand this idle taske,
And *Trinidados* smoke face vnmaske,
Who beeing but a swarie *Indian*,
Hath plaid the painted English *Curtesan*,
(Pitie: that so faire *Albions* worthie wits
Should fall into such furious frensy fits.)

But Nature, Loue, and my welwilling pen,
To Englands soile, and my deere Countrymen,
   Dutie and due allegiaunce binding band,
Hath forst mee take this idle taske in hand,
Which when it comes to the Iudiciall view,
Of the quicke sighted and refined Crew,
Of new enstalled Knights *Tabacconists*,
Of the sterne Censours Leering *Lucanists*,
I'm sure the one will wish the reeking fume,
That smoketh from his Nosthrils would Consume.
   Like fire and brimstone: my truth telling rimes,
(Such is the flintinesse of moderne times,)
Another teares my guiltlesse paper booke,
Hiding them in his bigge flops pocket nooke,
And at some publike shew in all mens sight,
With them hee kindles his his *Tabacco Pipe*,
They burne for *Heretiques*, (O foule Impietye,)
Cause they blasphemed *Tabaccos* Dietie.
   Let none denie but Iudies soile can yeeld,
The sou'raigne simples, of Apollos field.
Let England Spaine and the French *Fleur de Lis*
Let Irish Kerne and the Cold seated *Freese*
Confesse themselues in bourden dutie stand
To wholesome simples of *Guyana* land.
But hence thou Pagan Idol: tawnie weede,
Come not with-in our Fairie Costs to feede.
   Our wit-worne gallants, with the sent of thee,
Sent for the Deuill and his companie,
¶Go charme the Priest and Indian Canniballs,
That Cerimoniously dead sleeping falls,
Flat on the ground, by vertue of thy sent,

Then waking straight, and tells a wonderment,
Of strange euents and fearefull visions,
That he had seene in apparitions.
    Some swaggering gallants of great *Plutoes* Court,
I warrant you would he the truth report,
But would I were a Charmer for it sake,
In England it should little rest ytake,
O I would whip the queane with rods of steele,
That euer after she my ierks should feele.
And make hir sweare vppon my Charming hand,
Neuer t'set foot more on our Farie land.
    Pittie it is that smoking vanitie,
Is Englands most esteemed Curtesie.
Oft haue I heard it as an ould saide sawe,
The strong digesting hungrie Camells mawe,
Brooks stinging nettles and the vilest weeds,
That stinking dunghils in ranke plentie feeds.
But t'is a toye to mocke an Ape in deed,
That English men should loue a stranger weed.
    Oh crye you mercie now the cause I knowe,
It is *probatum* for the Pox I trow.
Peace tel-tale peace, blab not thy countries fault,
O seek to hide it in obliuions valt.
See if thou canst with arguments refraine,
The smokie humors of each wit-worne braine.
Then will I neuer looke for greater gaine,
Nor euer think my labour lost in vaine.

                                        J. H.

Eight Reasons and Arguments against Tobacco

or the dislike that I haue conceiued in the vse and practise of *Tabacco*, I take it to be grounded on eight principall reasons and arguments.

First, that in their vse or custome, no methode of order is obserued. Diuersitie and distinction of persons, tymes and seasons considered, no varietie of accidents and diseases pondered.

Secondly, for that it is in qualitie and complexion more hot and drye then may be conueniently vsed dayly of any man: much lesse of the hot and cholericque constitution.

Thirdly, for that it is experimented and tryed to be a most strong and violent purge.

Fourthly, for that it withereth and drieth vp naturall moisture in our bodies, therby causing sterrilitie and barrennesse: In which respect it seemeth an enemie to the continuaunce and propagacion of mankinde.

Fiftly, for that it decayeth and dissipateh naturall heate, that kindly warmeth in vs, and thereby is cause of crudities and rewmes, occasions of infinit maladies.

Sixtly, for that this herb or rather weed, seemeth not voide of venome and poison, and thereby seemeth an enemie to the lyfe of men.

Seauenthly, for that the first author and finder hereof was the Diuell, and the first practisers of the same were the Diuells Priests, and therefore not to be vsed of vs Christians.

Last of all, because it is a great augmentor of all sorts of melancholie in our bodies, a humor fit to prepare our bodies to receaue the prestigations and hellish illusions and impressions of the Diuell himselfe: in so much that many Phisitions and learned men doe hold this humour to be the verie seate of the Diuell in bodies possessed.

A Warning for
Tabacconists

THE FIRST REASON

ouching the first; Where no method
or order is vsed, ther resteth in all ar-
tes and other actions humaine, naught
else but dissolation and confusion,
a thing, as in the Common weale it is
pernicious, so in the preseruation of mans health it
hath been alwaies adiudged most dangerous.

But that in these our daies, in this land of *England*, this new come simple of the *West* commonly
knowne with vs by the name of *Tabacco*: is without all method and order of most men receiued,

43

may be apparant by this, that it is taken early in the morning, and also very late at night: in the morning fasting, and in the euening feasting and on a full stomacke. In the beginning, middle, and ende of meales. To be short, at all times, at all houres, and of all persons, this *Indian* stranger most familiarly is receiued: for the smoake of *Tabacco* seemeth to the fauorits thereof at no time vnseasonable. Neither that it ought to bee tied to reasons and rules (being perhaps a thing in it selfe more irregular and vnreasonable) seeing that by experience (as they thinck) they haue found great good & profit by the vse therof.

They boast much of this their experience as a sufficient ground for this their disorder. But their experience not grounded on reason, but rather repugnant thereto, and contrary to commonsence also, is a motiue sufficient for the simple, but no way an argument for the wiser sort, to daunce after their vnsauory and vnpleasant *Tabacco pipe*.

Galen in his Comment on his first booke of *Hippocrates Aphorismes*: sheweth that the art of *Phisicke* standeth on two legges, *Reason* and *Experience*: Whereof if either bee wanting, the whole art is lame and maimed.

For as *Reason* without *Experience* is very vncertaine: so is *Experience* without *Reason* very perillous and dangeroes; especially in matters inwardly to be taken and receiued into mens bodies, the which as they are diuers and differing in nature and complection, so are they also diuersly in diet to bee ordered, and by farre contrary medicines in their sicknesses cured.

For Example.

The diet conuenient for youth, is no waies agreeable to old age: neither is that diet which is appropriat to elder yeeres, any way profitable to youthfull and growing age.

And bodies of temper dry, require things in nature and qualitie moist. But moist complections and maladies growing of superfluities of humours, are more commonly remedied by things of nature drying and disiccatiue. By which last meanes wee see by experience, that some diseased of the dropsie (no doubt a colde and moist affect) haue receiued great helpe by the frequent vse of this *Tabacco*. For the siccety, & dri'th of this simple, together with his heat, in a body hidropicall, hauing fit matter & great store of cold humors to worke vpon, doth no doubt in that respect further their health, and yet can it not be iustly inferred heere of, that *Tabacco* simply taken without respect of times, persons, sexe, age, temperament and disease, any waies to be either profitable or else commendable.

Also fasting and abstinence for meate is assigned by *Hippocrates* in his *Aphorismes*, for a good remedie against full and repleat bodies.

Abstinuisse decet nimium quibus humida membra,
humida desiccat corpora nempe fames.

But yet the same *Hippocrates* denieth that kinde of abstinence to bee any waies conueni-ent for growing yeeres, or for the sicke of feuers consuming, & for such as are not accustomed therevnto.

Humidior victus pueris paritero; suetis,
Conuenit, accensis corporibusq; febri.

Moreouer some bodies receiue helpe and ease by purging and euacuation, as the bodies of wres-tlers, & such as are come to the top and extreame height of fulnesse, of whom *Hippocrates* speaketh of in his 3. *Aphorisme* of his booke.

Ad summam veniens habitudo athletica molem
noxia, cum non quo progrediatur habet.
Vno namque statu cum non consistere possit,
est in deterius retro necesse ruat.
Vnde fit vt corpus confestim soluere possit,
quo poterit rursus conuenienter alt.

And yet the same author in his Aphorismes doth testifie, purges no way to bee conuenient for sound and healthie bodies: for saith hee,

Sana corpora difficulter purgantia medicamenta
ferunt, et cito a purgantibus exoluuntur.

And to be short, neither one nor the other rem-edy can in any respect preuaile, if it be applied out of his due time and season: for,

Temporibus medicina valet, data tempore prosunt,
et data non apto tempore vina nocent.

And truely as no one kinde of diet can fit all sorts of bodies: So no one kinde of remedie can aptly be applied to all maladies, no more then one shooe can wel serue all mens feete.

What reason therfore haue these *Tabacconists* (I pray you) to offer this their *Tabacco* after one and the selfe same order to all men, ages, and complections indifferently, making no scruple of the fitnesse of time, quality of the disease, or temperament of the person to whom they offer it.

What thing can be more absurd and phantasticall, then to minister one & the selfe same remedy to contrary & repugnant affects, hot & cold, dry and moist, emptie and repleat, acute and cronicall, which for the more part haue deeper rootes, and are of longer continuance, then can sodenly be blowne away with a puffe of a smokie *Tabacco* pipe, yea & some of them can hardly be remoued by the great paynes, care & cunning of the expert and learned in *Phisicke*: for,

Nonest in medico semper releuetur vt aeger
Interdum docta plus valet arte malum.

And yet these Tabacco fauorits hold no disease so incurable but that in some measure it receiueth either cure or ease by this *Tabacco*.

But I assure you many diseases being of themselues and their owne nature, light and of easie cure, may by the vntimely vse of this same, become altogether incurable, such are, the first step or degree to an *Heticke*, distemper of heat in the Liuer, oppilations of the Lungs, and such like.

And truely if nothing else should make one out of fancie with the vse of *Tabacco*, it might be sufficient for an equall iudge to thinck with himself how vnnaturall a thing it is to peruert the naturall vse & offices of the parts of the bodie, for by the force of *Tabacco* the mouth, throte, and stomacke, (appointed by nature for the receipt of food & nourishment for the whole body) are made emunctuary clensing places and sincks, (supplying heerein the office of the most abiect and basest part) for the filth and superfluous excrements of the whole body.

THE SECOND REASON

he second reason against the ordinarie vse of *Tabacco*, is taken from the excesse of his two manifest qualities of heat and dri'th, which Monardus and others also haue affirmed to come neere to the third degree of excesse in either qualitie.

So that if men of hot and dry constitution should often vse the feume of *Tabacco*, no doubt they should increase much their distemper, for like added to his like, increaseth the resemblance & similitude the more according to that *Axiome* in *Philosophie: Omnes simile additum simili reddia ipsum magis simile.* Whervpon Aristotle in his 8. booke and 29. Chap. *De animalibus,* inferreth, that a Snake if he eate of a Scorpion waxeth farre more venemous then he was before.

But I neede not to stand long vpon this point, seeing that daily practise & experience teachth vs, that heat increaseth heat, & things cold, do increase in vs a greater cold, the like may bee said of the other qualities of dri'th and moisture, so that in natural reason and common sence it seemeth true that the extreame & violent dri'th & heat of *Tabacco,* maketh it far vnfit & vnwholesome for thin & cholericke bodies. And so is it also for youth and such as grow, for *Qui crescunt plurimum habent innati caloris,*[1] this naturall heat in youth, by the immoderate vse of this fierie fume would soone turne vnto a heat vnnaturall, and thereby be occasion of infinite maladies.

But I hold it a thing very dangerous, not onely for the yonger sort, but also for all other ages and constitutions whatsoeuer, to bee ouer bold with *Tabacco.* For it doth not onely consume and dissipate naturall heat in them (by increasing of the vnnaturall) but it wasteth also & drieth vp radicall moisture (the principall subiect of natiue heat) so that heereof insueth in the bodie great store of

---

1   Those who grow have the most inborn heat. —Ed.

crud & vndigested humours, the effects of immoderate heat in vs.

For it is not fierie nor immoderate heat in vs, but rather a milde & vnctuous warmth, consisting in a temerate & moderate moisture that performeth as well concoction as all other naturall actions in vs.

Which thing is very apparant & conspicuous in such as are afflicted with hot & burning Feuers: In whom as the fierie heat appeareth most, so crude and vndigested humours doe abound more then in such as are cleare of such extremitie of heates. Neither doe their humors at any time come to perfect digestion in them, vntill the rigor and violence of that fierie heate be in some sort (by cooling diet and medicine) repressed.

Much lesse therefore are the patrons of *Tabacco* to bee beeleeued in this, that hot and burning Agues (rising of corruption and putrefaction of choler & blood in the veines or about the principall parts of mans bodie) may bee cured with an infusion of Tabacco lease in white Wine steeped all night.

For as it was euer an aphorisme & maxime in Phisicke, that as like is maintayned by his like, So was it also of like certaintie in the same art, that *Contraria a contrarijs currantur.* Contraries are cured by their contraries. I meane contrary rather to the disease, or to the cause of the disease.

But what contrarietie I pray you can be found betweene *Tabacco* and a Feuer tercian or burning Ague: When as they manifestly agree in their principall qualities of heate and dri'th: both equally falling in excesse of either of them? The like may be said of other effects proceeding of the same of like causes.

But to let the diseased passe, and to come to those which are of perfect health, I take it very dangerous and hurtfull for them often to vse this *Tabacco* for therby great part of that humour is dissipated, wasted, spent & cast foorth of the body by often vomits, seeges, swets and continnall spittings and coughings, which in processe of time would turne to good blood, and holsome nurrishment for the bodie.

For Crude and watrish humors (which for the most part are all those which by this medicine are) are oftentimes very necessary for many vses in the body: As for pliant motion of the Ioints, and principally for nurrishment of the flegmaticke and colder parts.

And it is a receiued opinion amongst the best *Phisitions* that nature (being a prouident & carefull nurce of mankinde) hath purposely left this Crudie humour in our bodyes, to the intent that we might euer haue some thing in store to nourish vs, if happely we should at any time want other foode.

But that no small part of our nurishment is drawne away by the vntimely vse of this *Tabacco*, may manifestly appeare by those men, who before the vse thereof were grose and foggy, but after they haue acquainted themselues with this kinde of practise, they became very leane and slender.

So that no doubt, if they desist not in time from farther vse therof, ther is no small suspition least that they shall therby fall into Consumptions, & to that of the most dangerous sorts called of the Phisition, Marasmos proceding of want of substanciall nurrishment, & dissipation of naturall heat and decay of spirits in the body.

And heerein I cannot but wonder much at the ouer sight of some, who otherwise being learned and wise, yet in this seeme very Paradoxicall, when as they contend to proue Tabacco to be a great nurrisher. For beesides that, it is manifest that it taketh away great part of our nurrishment, by the extreame euacuation it procureth, it is also (by meanes of his great heat & drynesse) very vnapt to breed any good nurishment in vs.

To this may bee added, his vnpleasaunt and vngratefull smell, insomuch that the tasters thereof beare away with them in their bodyes and breath, the loathsome *Tabacco* sent, long time after.

So that it is very euident and manifest that as well in respect of his substance (ouer hot & dry) as also of his vnpleasing & stinking sent, it is neither fit to nurish the humerall & solide parts, nor yet apt to refresh & comfort the spirits of man, be they naturall in the Liuer, vitall in the hart, or sensible or animall in the braine and sinewes. For as touching the humours in vs, they are aptest nourished by such things as are either humorall and moist, or else, may easely bee turned and conuerted into a liquid and thin substance.

And as for the hard and solede parts of the body as bones, sinewes, vaines & artires) they cannot receiue any nutriment of any thing before it bee first turned into some moist and liquid substance also, apt to be suked & drunck into the former parts, & afterward by the force of natures worke, assimulated, hardened, & transformed into the very nature & substance of the parts by it nurished. But as for the spirits, it hath ben a question much disputed on amongst the *Philosophers*, (as *Aristotle*, *Plato*, and others) of old time, & their expositers since; whether smels or odours may any wayes nourish the same. And (if I be not deceiued) they all agree in this, that mens spirits doe feele great comfort and refreshing by such sweet and pleasant sauours as are founded & subiected in some moyst & vnctuous matter. But this priuiledge cannot in any respect bee graunted to *Tabacco*, both for that hir sauour is very vnsauorie & stincking, & also because it is placed & founded in a very dry and withered substance. Insomuch as that the tasters and drinckers thereof, thincke it not fit to bee taken, vntill it bee thoroughly parched and dryed, that thereby it might the better receiue the force of the fire, & the sooner be kindled therwith.

Now that sweet and pleasant sauours & delightfull fumes, doe greatly refresh our spirits and recreate the sences, it is euidently perceiued by our vsuall practise: When to the feeble and languishing persons, and to such as faint or sound, we presently offer them the sent of Rosewater mixed with a little vineger, that it might the more speedely peirce; and the sicke person feeleth great comfort thereby.

But on the contrary, stincking & filthie smels, are so far from refreshing vs, as that they vtterly extinguish & quell our spirits in vs; and to some procure hastie and vntimely deaths, (or at the least some vncurable maladies and loathsome diseases).

Ambrose Parve,[2] a *French Chirurgion* not vnlearned, & in his profession most expert, reporteth of himselfe in the 12. Chapter of his treatise of the plague, that visiting a certaine pacient of his, that had by meanes of the plague a botch in his flancke or groyne, and other blanes elsewhere in his body: Whilst rashly hee vnfolded the bed clothes, the better to take view of the sores, hee was sodainely stroke into a sound with the stincke & loathsome breath that steymed from these vlcers, & perced vp to his braine through his nosthrils, in such sort as that he hardly recouered his life. Afterward being recalled to his sence & feeling againe, hee thought the house wherled round, & had fallen sodenly downe againe, if happely he had not taken better holde of the bed post, and stayed himselfe.

How noysome and irkesome a thing vnpleasant and stincking sauours be to the braynes of men may easely bee coniectured by the vsuall custome of most men, who neuer passe by any vnsauory place, but they streight wayes stop their noses & mouthes with their hands or other meanes, least

2   Ambroise Paré (c. 1510 – 1590). —Ed.

that the ill vapor or stench therof should any waies offend or loath their braine.

But to come to our *Tabacco*, if any man doubt of his ill sauour & bad sent, I refer him to the report of those, who haue had longest tryall therof. No doubt, except they be altogether shamelesse, they will truely informe him therof. I remember that being called once to the cure of an honorable Earle now departed this life, amongst other learned and expert *Phisitions*, there hapned one to be called, who as in times past he was *Chimicall*, so in the vntimely vse of this plant he seemed to bee ouer fantasticall. It fortuned the very morning that he came vnto his Honors presence, he had (according to his accustomed wont) taken his mornings draft of *Tabacco*, with the fume wherof, he so perfumed his Lordships bedchamber in such sort, as that the Earle being meruaylous anoyed therwith, told me after the departure of the former Phisition, that from thence foorth hee had rather lose the benefit of that mans counsell in Phisicke, then to indure such a horrible a fume againe. This good being demaunded of other *Phisitions*, (wherof two were hir Maiesties) the present, what reason he had for this his custome? answered that he would not but for 100 pounds he had vsed this feume at first, for thereby he found great ease for his cold reumatick & stomacke. But now said he, I would that I could so easely leaue it, condicionallie I had giuen 300 pounds more, for I finde my selfe hart sick that day, till I haue tasted thereof.

No doubt the long and dailie vse of drincking *Tabacco*, had accustomed his stomack to draw to it watrish and rewmetick matter in great aboundance, the quantitie wherof, vrged nature to seeke meanes for the expelling the same againe, which could, by no other thing be more fitly performed then by *Tabacco* it selfe.

For as it hath a powre & faculty to draw to the stomacke, (as other strong purges haue) so likewise hath it a property and vertue to expell forth the same, no otherwise then all other purges haue. But heerein it differeth from other purges, that it seemeth to be of a far more thin & subtile nature then other purges bee, by meanes wherof, nature is so pricked and forced oftentimes in such violent sort, as that it causeth violent euacuation, as well by stoole vomits and swetes, as also by saliuacion, coughing & spittings, which thing other purges vsually doe not, albeit they be very forceable, violent and strong.

So that heereof is gathered the fourth reason beefore aleadged, that *Tabacco* is not familiarly to be vsed beecause it is a vehement and violent purge.

The Third Reason

neede not stand long on this point, to proue *Tabacco* to bee a strong and violent purge: for that in daily practise & common experience the same is most euident and manifest to most men. And to doubt of that which of it selfe is perspicuous, were grose stupiditie, and to denie that which is to our sence most cleere and euident, were a point next to extreame folly.

The often scowrings, fluxes, vomets, swetes, and other immoderate euacuations insident to this simple, doe testifie the same to purge most violently.

Furthermore, *Tabacco* is found to be of that strength & force, that the verie maceration or infusion of one leafe thereof in white wine ouernight doth procure strong and extreame vomits.

It is as yet fresh in memorie, that diuers yong Gentlemen, by the daylie vse of this *Tabacco*, haue brought themselues to flixes and disenteries, and of late at *Bath* a Scholler of some good accompt and worshipfull calling, was supposed to haue perished by this practise, for his humours beeing sharpened and made thin by the frequent vse of *Tabacco*, after that they had once taken a course downward, they ran in such violence, as that by no Art or Phisicks skill they could be stayed, till the man most miserably ended his life, being then in the verie prime and vigour of his age.

But no purge, (be he familiar or gentle, or else violent and hurtfull) ought by the rules of Phisicke to bee familiarly and daily vsed of any man that hath respect either of his life, or regard to his health.

For as concerning such as are in perfect health *Hippocrates* the Prince of *Phisitions* in the 36. *Aphorisme* of his second booke affirmeth: *Corpora si per medicamenta purgantur exoluuntur celeriter; & quae prauo cibo vtuntur.* Sound and healthie bodies (sayth he) soone wast and consume, by the vse of purging medicines. In like case doe they which feede on corrupt and vnwholesome meates.

Likewise the same author in the 37. *Aphorisme* of the former booke, sayth, that *Qui corpora habent commoderata iis purgationes difficiles sunt.* To such as are in health purging medicines are very dangerous. And truely this his assertion seemeth to be grounded vpon good & substanciall reason. For wheras the vertue and operacion of the purge is to draw & expell foorth of the body such corrupt & vnholsome humours as haue any affinitie or likenesse in substance with the purge; & in healthy bodyes finding none of that disposition & nature, the purge then either loseth his operation and action, & therby is conuerted into some bad humour in the bodie, or else it draweth and expelleth foorth humours very profitable & necessary for the nurrishment and sustentation of the body. And therefore all purges must needes bee to sound and healthy bodyes very perillous and dangerous.

And as for sicke and diseased men, they ought onely to vse purging remedies at such times as their bodies and humours shall be made fit and apt for the operation of the purge, according to that counsell of *Hippocrates* in his tenth *Aphorisme* of his second booke, saying:

> *Purganti quoties vacuæ medicamine corpus,*
> *quo bene res Cedat, fluxile redde prius.*

So often as thou purgest, so often also ought you to make your bodies apt thereto, and the humours (to be purged) fluxible, that the parts and passages of the body being open, and the humours apt to runne, the purgation might worke with lesse torments and griefe to the partie purged.

So that it seemeth very apparant true, that neither in health, nor yet in sicknesse, that so vntimely and vulgar vse of *Tabacco* (beeing before prooued a violent purge) can be vsed without great hurt and danger.

Neither ought this kind of remedie to be giuen at anytime, but in causes of extremitie, and in desperate diseases onely. For that it is an extreame and desperate medicine. *Extremis enim morbis extrema remedia adhibedasunt,* saith our *Hippocrates*. And in his comment vpon the same *Aphorisme*, sheweth all strong purges to be reckoned amongst extreame remedies.

THE FOURTH REASON

he fourth argument against this new-come simple, was that it drieth vp and withereth our vnctuous and radicall moisture in vs, and therby seemeth an vtter enemie to the continuance and propagation of mankinde. This may be prooued in this sort.

That thing which depriueth the body of norishment and foode, doth also wither & dry vp our naturall and radical moisture; (because this hath his refreshing and sustentation from the purest part of the blood ingendred of our nourishments). But *Tabacco* was shewed before to depriue vs our norishment, in that it spendeth and euacuateth out of vs by spitting and sweats & otherwise much of that matter that in time would proue in vs good blood & good foode for our bodies. And therefore *Tabacco* must needs be said to be a great decaier and witherer of our radicall moysture before specified.

Moreouer *Tabacco* by meanes of his great heat and immeasurable drinesse, dissipateth naturall heate and kinde warm'th in our bodies, and thereby is cause of defect of good concoction & perfect disgestion in vs. The humors therfore in vs by this meanes made crude and rawe, can be no fit aliment or nutriment for the vnctuous and substantiall humiditie, wherin with moderate and kindly heate the Philosopher esteemed the life of man to consist.

And last of all, wheras the sperme & seed of man, is supposed (by the Phisitians & natural Philosophers also) to be framed of the purest & finest part of his blood by the action & vertue of kindly warm'th working therin; the blood being now vndigested & crude, and the naturall heate peruerted & corrupted by the immoderate vse of this hellish smoake, reeking foorth of *Plutoes* forge, what sperme or seed shall we expect to come from them that daily vse or rather shamefully abuse this so apparant an enemy to the propagation therof, as wel if you respect the materiall cause of seed consisting in the perfectest & most concocted parts of the blood) as his efficient (resting in the moderation of naturall heat) both greatly altered and decayed by the vse of *Tabacco*.

Hereby it must needs in consequent follow, that the continuation & propagation of mankinde (consisting principally in his perfect & vncorrupt seed) is in these men much abridged.

And for certaine proofe that *Tabacco* dryeth vp the sperme & seed of man, I heare by faithfull relation of such as haue much vsed it; That whereas before the vse thereof, they had bene long molested with a fluxe of seed, commonly called with vs the running of the reines, and of the Phisitian *Gomorrhaea*, (proceeding in them by reason of great quantitie & abundance of that matter seeking vent forth of the bodie) they were in short space eased of this affect by the onely vse of this medicine. For no doubt, this fierie fume, dried vp the superfluitie of that matter, which by reason of her thin and great quantitie, easily dropped from them. But if they persist ouer long in the practise therof, no doubt more of that spermaticall humiditie wil be dried vp in them, the will be conuenient for their health, or for the increase of their like; wherby the propogation & continuation of mankind in this world must need be abridged.

THE FIFTH REASON

he fifth argument against *Tabacco* was, that it dissipateth naturall heate, and thereby was occasion of rawe and vndigested humours in the bodie.

This thing in part hath bene demonstrated before in the chapter precedent, to which may here be added, that where naturall and kind heat is by any meane made more violent and fiery, there the parts of the body are made more hard and dried, and thereby the more vnfit and vnapt to drinke or receiue into them such liquid and moist matter, as by the daily foode should accrue and grow to them. Wherevpon it falleth forth, that that humiditie that should bee conuerted into the nature & substance of the sollide parts, is made (by meanes of their not admission thereof) excrementall and superfluous.

For it is not a thing either strange or absurd in Philosophie, that things of qualitie drie, may by an

accidentall meanes, be cause of superfluous moisture. We see this thing confirmed by *Galen* himself, in his second booke and second Chapter, *De
temperamentis*, and also by *Auicen*.

We see by experience, that old persons being
naturally drie in their sollide parts, and haue for
that cause, their skin parched, their faces withered, their sinewes stiffe, their backes stouping,
and yet who doubteth but such persons haue in
their intrailes and inward parts, great store of
flegmaticke and excrementall moistures, proceeding of want of good digestian and concoction
in those parts.

And truly those superfluities do the more
abound in them, for that their firme and sollide
parts (as Sinewes, Bones, & Flesh, Veines, Artiers,
and Ligaments) are too drie and hard to receiue
and sucke vp so much of that alimentall humour
which Nature dooth daily send to them for their
sustenance and reliefe.

And hereof is seene in daily experience, that
olde folk are troubled most with rewmes, Catar-
res, coughs, spatterings, vomits, scourings, and
such like.

And that old age is naturally drie and hard, Galen declareth in these words: *Senum temperies
sicca est, pro exemplo sunt arbores, Nāquoties se-
nescunt magis exiccantur.*

We see also that the earth in Haruest time being
ouer dried and parched with the heate of the Som-
mers Sunne, cannot so speedily suck and drinke vp

such sudden showres of raine, as at that time most vsually doo happen.

And therefore about that time of the yeare we see the greatest land flouds to appeare, and most harmes to happen to men by losse of their Hey carried away thereby.

All which proceedeth by reason of the great siccetie and dri'th of the earth at that season, causing it to be far vnapt to receiue that sudden moisture flowing on the face thereof.

In like case the firme and sollide parts of mans body, being ouer drie and hardned by the long and continuall vse of *Tabacco*, do with the more difficultie receiue and imbybe into them the alimentall humiditie before specified: and therfore they remaine more copious in the body.

The Sixth Reason

he sixt Reason against *Tabacco* was, that this Plant seemeth not voyd of suspition of a venemous and poysoned nature, and therefore ought not so carelessly or confidently to be vsed.

The venemous and poisoned substance and nature of *Tabacco*, is manifested and prooued by this, that it is daily experimented, and before was prooued by vs, to be a violent and most forceable purge.

Galen in his second booke *De ratione virtus*, and 12. Section, holdeth for a certaintie that all vehement and violent purges, haue in them some deliterious & poysoned nature, & a facultie or operation cleane contrary to the nature of man.

And in the sixt of his Epidenickes, the same *Galen* affirmeth, that in times past purging medicines were esteemed deliterious, for that they (being taken in any large quantitie) were offensiue to nature, destroying and wasting the same.

In good Authors I finde three kinds of deliterious medicines. The one in manifest qualitie, either excessiue hote, as *Calcanthum*, or else extreame cold (as *Mandrake*) or *Opium*.

Of the second sort, are those which by their owne poysoned nature and substance, be deadly offensiue to the takers therof, and they being receiued but in small dose or quantitie, kill and poyson the takers thereof. Such are venemous musrumps, *Napellum*, *Taxicum*, and such like.

Of the third kind of deliterious and deadly medicines, be such, as are by reason of their vehement & violent euacuation, most daungerous and perillous, if in any large quantitie they be assumed. Such be *Enphorbium*, *Praecipitate*, *Eleterium*, and *Tabacco* it selfe.

Which last as it is deliterious by violent euacuation, So it is also very pernicious and hurtfull *in his manifest and euident qualities of extreame dry'th and heate included therein.*

But touching his violent euacuation and purging qualitie, it hath bene sufficiently shewed before. This one thing may be added therevnto, that

Tabacco is in this respect more perillous, for that it is taken without due preparation and correction.

For it is confessed of all Phisitians, that euery purging medicine if it be strong (in respect of the deliterious & bad qualitie it hath) ought to be artificially corrected before it be taken, least he communicate his bad and venemous nature, to the stomack & inward parts.

Herevpon it is a vsuall custome in Phisicke, to mix with purges, Mastich, Cloues, Cinamome, Ginger, Aniseeds, Nutmegs, and such like sweete and aramaticall Spices, partly to take away the vngratefull sent of the purge, and partly to defend the vitall spirits, & principall parts, from the malice and hurt which otherwise would happen by the ill qualitie of the purge.

Out of this rule of preparation of purges, onely *Aloes Succotrine* is by *Mesnes* excepted. Which as hee affirmeth) is so farre from ill qualitie and deliterious nature, as that it is commonly giuen with other purges to amend & correct their venemous & malitious nature.

But what correctiues I pray you in our time and Countrey are there vsed in this Indian *Tabacco*, which the more simple & sincere it is, the more holsome and effectuall it is adiudged to be? And if it haue by any meanes any aramaticall spices shufled amongst it, it is straight reiected and condemned for naught & counterfeit.

I denie not but that since *Hippocrates* and *Mesnes* time, there haue beene found out sundrie purges by the latter Arabians, which for that they worke gently and without offence, are called of them, *Benedicta Medicamenta*: Blessed and safe medicines, and therefore haue need of no preparation to be vsed with them for their correction. Such are thought to be *Manna* of *Calabria*, *Camarinds*, *Cassia* of *Rhubarbe*. But this *Tabacco* (now in vse) is of an other keye, and no waies to be accounted *Benedictum* in working, but rather diabolicall and hellish: for that it worketh with extremitie, torments and griefe.

And that it is also in substance and nature deliterious and venemous, may be gathered by the symtornes and accidents which doo immediately follow and ensue the large drinking therof. That are, violent vomits, many and infinite stooles, great gnawings and torments in the guts and inward parts. Coldnesse in the outward and externall members, Crampes, Convultions, cold sweats, ill colour, and wannesse of skinne, defect of feeling, sence, & vnderstanding, losse of sight, giddinesse of the head and braine, profound and deep sleepe, faintnesse, sounding, and to some hastie and vntimely death. All which, or the most part of them concurring, do manifest a poisoned qualitie or venemous nature in the thing receiued.

And it is the more daungerous for that it hath in it the effects of contrary and repuguant poisons: for albeit it be in qualitie very hotte & drie, yet hath it a stupifying and benumming effect, not much vnlike to Opium or Henbane: which ere held to be colde in the extreamest degree. And albeit, it be apt to suffocate or strangle like to Gipsum or playster of Parrise, yet doth it purge & scoure as violently as Precipatate or Quick-siluer sublymed.

I cannot resemble the poysoned force of this *Tabacco* to any thing more aptly, then to the venome of a Scorpion, which neuer receiueth cure but from the Scorpion it selfe, bruised or annointed on the place stung. In like case the venemous impression left in the stomacke by *Tabacco*, receiueth no ease by any thing else whatsoeuer, but by *Tabacco* onely, eftsoone reiterated and resumed. This onely difference seemeth to be betweene these two poysons, That the venome of the Scorpion hath his perfect and absolute cure from the Scorpion it selfe, but that of *Tabacco* hath onely a certaine ease and paliation for a time by the fume of *Tabacco* receiued; but after perfect and absolute cure, this Tabacco by it selfe a thousand times resumed or reiterated, admitteth none.

Neither do I take it of great importance which is by some alleaged; That many here in *England* do take the fume of *Tabacco* without hurt or inconuenience, and without any such strange accidents following. For the custome of taking *Tabacco* with vs, is in that maner, as that, it neither profiteth, nor yet hurteth much.

For what great inconuenience (I pray you) can happen to the taker thereof, when as he receiuing it at the mouth, doth straightway puffe it forth againe, or snuffeth it out at his nostrels, before it can haue sufficient time and space, to imprint his malicious and venemous qualitie in their bodies?

Fewe or none do take it downe their throates, and such as let it passe down, they mince it in such sort, and swallow it in so small quantitie, as that no great detriment can happen to them thereby.

But if happily any, more audacious then circumspect, shall let downe any large quantitie thereof, then shal you euidently perceiue in him, most of those accidents before specified.

I am not ignorant that many perillous and deadly poysons are sometimes taken into the body without offence and daunger, but then they are either in very small quantitie (as I spake before) or else so repressed and corrected with other Cordialls, as that they cannot offend, but sometimes they bring great commoditie and profit with them.

For example, the flesh of Vipers in Treacle is so tempered and corrected, that it profiteth much to such as orderly reciue it, against any poyson or contagion whatsoeuer. And quick-siluer well mortified, is often giuen, & inwardly taken, against many infirmities, with good successe.

So in like maner we denie not but that in smal quantitie *Tabacco* may be taken of any men without peril or imminent danger, & especially being corrected & purified by the force of the fire wherewith it is ministred.

For that fire sometimes doth represse the poisoned vapour of venemous things, may be prooued by the testimony of *Seneca*, who (in his 2. booke

of his natural questions, and 31. Chapter, going
about to shewe the reason why that poisoned and
venemous beasts do neuer engender wormes within them, vntill such time as they be first striken
with lightning) saith, that wormes are engendred
of humours apt to receiue life. But such be farre
differing from such as are of a venemous or poisoned disposition or nature, for they are altogether aduersaries and enemies to life. This poisoned
and venemous nature in Serpents (once striken
with lightning) is in them wasted, dissipated & dis-
pearced, by meanes of the fire in the lightning, and
the humors remaining after in them, beeing freed
from venome and poison, may the more aptly be
conuerted into things bearing life, and to wormes
themselues.

It may also be assigned out of *Mercurialis* for an
other reason, why wormes are not engendered in
poisoned serpents, because that wormes haue their
originall from vndigested and crudie humours in
the body: *But Serpents haue no such in them: for
all their humours be well and perfectly digested.*
Which may well bee gathered by the fragrant and
sweete smell, and pleasant smell and sent, which
breathing from their bodies, is left behind in those
places where they vsually haunt.

But here may be obiected, that if *Tabacco* were
of that poysoned nature (as wee haue affirmed)
then no doubt, the Indians (who vsually drinke
it) should haue long since bin poisoned therewith. But hitherto they haue found no such hurt,

but rather great commoditie and manifest benefit thereby. As appeareth by *Monardus* in his Treatise of *Tabacco*.

To this may be answered, that the oddes and diuersitie of their bodies and humours from ours, may alter much the case. Or else, that long custome and familiar vse of this *Tabacco* from their infancie, hath confirmed their bodies, to suffer & endure the same without hurt or offence: for custome altereth nature.

In like case I read in *Galen* in his 3. booke of simples, and 18. Chap. of a certain old woman that nourished her selfe long season with poisoned Hemlockes. *By litle and litle* (saith he) *shee accustomed nature thereto, that at length, this poyson became familiar to her, and no way offensiue, but rather nourishing to her body.*

Auicen also in his Treatise *de Viribus Cordis*, alleaging *Rufus* an auncient Phisitian for his authour, reporteth that there was a yong maid, who being fed & norished long time with poyson, liued her self in perfect health. And yet with her venemous breath she poysoned and infected all other persons that came neare to the same.

Plynie in his 7. booke & 2. chap. of his naturall history. And *Aulue Gellius, noct. attic. 16. cap. 11.* And *Siluius Italicus* in 8. *lib.* doo all testifie that in times past there were certain people in *Italy* (Marsitians by name) who vsually handled and sold, yea and fed on also the flesh of Vipers. Which of all Serpents are accounted most malignant and venemous.

And *Virgil* in his 7. *Aeneid.* faineth those people to be the ofspring of *Circes*, and that they had a naturall gift giuen them by her, to tame & enchaunt that kind of Serpent: and also to qualifie & delay the venemous and poysoned nature thereof.

Of these men *Galen* maketh mention in his 11. booke of simple medicines, where he confesseth, that being at *Rome*, he inquired diligently of those people (tearmed *Marsi*) of the nature & qualitie of vipers, and how they differed from the other Serpent called *Dipsas*. Because (saith he) they were expert and cunning in them.

So that it is manifest & apparant by the testimonies before rehearsed, that custome may alter & change nature and the qualitie of things, according to that vsuall *Consuetude alterat naturā.* Custom changeth nature, & at length turneth into nature it self; for it is an other nature.

The like is seene in the East *Indies*, where the Turkes familiarly vse *Opium* in large quantitie, which to vs but in very small dose is experimented to be manifest poyson: onely long vse & familiar practise hath made this vnconuenient for their bodies.

And so no doubt if our countrey men from their infancie had by litle and litle vsed to take this *Tabacco* fume or other poyson whatsoeuer, they should haue had as litle cause to feare the daunger thereof, as the Turkes haue of their Opium, or the old Marsitians had of Vipers, or the West Indians haue of their *Tabacco*. But for want of that Custome, it fareth with vs in that sort, that if we take any great quantitie of the *Opium* before specified, we shall rather die on the sudden, or else fall into that kinde of dead sleepe, as that we shall by no other meanes then by the Arch-angels trumpet (sounding at the latter day) be awakened thereout.

To this may be added a secret vertue and specificall qualitie giuen the Indians by nature, whereby they are not ouercome by this kinde of poyson, as other Nations be. For *Sextus Empericus* reporteth in the like case, that one *Attienagoras Argivus* had a gift giuen by nature euen from his birth, that hee could bee hurt by no venemous Beast or Serpent whatsoeuer. And that certaine people of *Aethiopia* did naturally feed & nourish themselues with the flesh of Scorpions.

But we Englishmen may not safely presume that this specifical vertue & hidden qualitie doth abide or lurk in vs, seeing that by far weaker poisons then these, we sustaine infinit perils, and often incurre death it selfe.

Wherefore we haue the lesse cause to venture on things in reason suspected to be of a venemous & poysoned qualitie, because forsoothe the Indians doo it without offence.

Neither is it of any great waight or moment which is alleadged of the *Tabacco* patrons for her commendation, that Marriners and Sea-faring men, neuer found any remedie so forceable against the Scuruie and other diseases of like nature, commonly incident to that kinde of people (by meanes of the foggy ayre in the Sea, and their vnholsome diet) then is the fume of *Tabacco*.

The reason of this profit in Marriners may bee, because their bodies after long lying on the Seas, are filled and stuffed with badde and corrupt humours, on the which the force and power of *Tabacco* dooth worke, drawing and purging them forth of the body, no otherwise then other strong purges expell and purge forth such corrupt humours as haue any similitude or likenesse to themselues.

But as strong purges taken of sound and holsome bodies (as I shewed you before) be very perillous and dangerous: So truly is *Tabacco*, being taken of such as are cleare and voyd of such impure and corrupt matter, which to the Marriners is most familiar and vsuall.

The like is seene of other poysons, which when they find any of their owne qualitie & nature in mans body, or that hath any likenesse or similitude to them, they drawe forth the same (the like couering his like) and leaue the sound and healthy humours cleare and vnspotted.

But when no such poisoned matter is found in the bodie, then dooth the poyson or venome receiued, worke on the good humours, vtterly corrupting and destroying them. So that it is apparant that sometime venomes (to venemous and poysoned persons) may be profitable & medicinable. But to sound & healthy bodies they can neuer happen without danger.

THE SEVENTH REASON

he seuenth reason against *Tabacco* was, that this hearbe seemed to bee first found out and inuented by the diuell, and first vsed and practised by the diuels priests, and therfore not to be vsed of vs Christians.

That the diuell was the first author hereof, *Monardus* in his Treatise of *Tabacco* dooth sufficiently witnesse, saying,[3] The Indian Priests (who no doubt were instruments of the diuell whom they serue) doo euer before they answere to questions propounded to them by their Princes, drinke of this *Tabacco* fume, with the vigour and strength wherof, they fall suddenly to the ground, as dead men, remaining so, according to the quantitie of the smoake that they had taken. And when the hearbe had done his worke, they reuiue and wake, giuing answeres according to the visions and illusions which they saw whilst they were wrapt in that order.

And they interpreted their demaunds as to them seemed best, or as the diuell had counselled them, giuing continual doubtful answers, in such sort, that howsoeuer they fell out, they might turne it to their purpose, like vnto the Oracle of *Apollo*. As

---

3   The period here has been changed to a comma, as the author seems to be quoting or paraphrasing Monardus in what follows. —Ed.

Aio te Æacide Romanos vincere posse.

Which might be vnderstood, that either he might ouerthrow the Romanes, or that the Romanes might ouercome him.

But yet in more plaine words, the same *Monardus* litle after declareth the Diuell to bee the author of *Tabacco*, and of the knowledge thereof, saying: And as the Diuell is a deceiuer, and hath the knowledge of the vertue of hearbes; so hee did shewe them the vertue of this hearbe, by meanes whereof they might see the imaginations and Visions that hee representeth vnto them, and by that meanes dooth deceiue them.

Wherfore in mine opinion this practise is the more to be eschued of vs Christians, who follow & professe Christ as the onely veritie and truth, and detest and abhorre the diuell, as a lyar and deceiuer of mankinde.

THE EIGHTH AND LAST REASON

he last, and that not the least argument against *Tabacco*, was that it is a great encreaser of melancholy in vs, and thereby disposeth our bodies to all melancholy impressions and effects proceeding of that humour.

Galen in his second booke of temperaments and 3. Chapter, defineth Melancholy to be the very sediment and dregges of bloud; which is so farre thicker & colder then bloud, as yeallow choller is held to be thinner and hotter then the same.

And this melancholy humour is said to bee of two sorts: the one naturall, the other vnnaturall.

The naturall is that thicke part of the bloud before rehearsed. The vnnaturall is not the sediment or grounds of good bloud, but rather a certain burnt and parched matter rising of the adustian and scorching of the other humors, that is, of phlegme, yealow choller, and of the former sediment of pure bloud, which we termed naturall melancholy.

And albeit it seemeth very vnlike that phlegme (being of nature cold and moist) may be any adustian be turned into swoart and blacke choller; yet in qualitie and disposition that humour doth often represent and resemble melancholy it selfe. And therefore *Galen* holdeth sometimes melancholy to bee ingendered of phlegmy ouerhardned and dried.

The contrarietie and diuersitie of these vnnaturall melancholies, doth hang and depend on the contrarietie and difference of the humours whereof they bee engendered.

All these sorts of melancholies are augmented and encreased much in such as often accustome themselues to the fume of *Tabacco*.

For first, touching the natural melancholy, it is manifest that the thicker and grosser that the bloud is, the more of that thicke and earthly sediment it shall containe. But *Tabacco* thickeneth and engrosseth the bloud, and therefore *Tabacco* engendereth in vs a greater store of that thicke and grosse sediment which wee defined to bee of *Galen* called naturall melancholy.

The Maior or first Proposition is manifest, for all liquid and moist things are the more thicke, or thinne, and cleare, according to the quantitie of the grounds and feces mixed in the same. For if the groundes be many, then is the matter or humor troublesome and thicke. But if the dregges or feces be fewe, then is the humor cleare and thin.

The Minor or second Proposition of the former Sillogisme, may be proued in this sort. All those things which waste and consume the purest & thinnest parts of the blood, doo cause the same blood to remaine afterward more grosse and thicke, and therfore may iustly be said to thicken the blood.

But *Tabacco* wasteth and absumeth the liquid and thin part of our blood, and therfore *Tabacco* may iustly be said to thicken the same. The Maior Proposition being euident, needeth no farther proofe.

The Minor is prooued by daily and vsuall practise and experience of such as commonly doo drinke this Tabacco. For thereby doo they purge great store of a cleare and thin humour, which would mixe it selfe with the blood, and cause the same to be more liquid and fluent, and in time also (by good Concoction) turne into pure and subtile blood, apt to feede and nourish the bodie.

And albeit melancholy (being of nature cold) seemeth to haue no need of phlegmetique and thin humours to be mixed therewith (least that his colde distemper be greatly increased thereby): yet of necessitie some store of this crude and rawe matter is required to runne with the melancholy Iuice, to moderate and temper his extreame siccetie and drythe, and to defend it from Induration & hardnesse. The increase whereof in our bodies, breedeth dulnesse, sottishnesse, and blockishnesse. All which are the vsuall effects of ouer-hardened and dryed melancholie.

For melancholy ouer-hardened, if it come once to be cooled, it is extreame cold as Iron. Which being heat, is extreame hotte; and being cooled againe, is extreame cold also.

So this hard and drie melancholy once depriued of naturall heate by the inordinate vse of *Tabacco* fewme (the fierie heate of the one dissipating the naturall and lesser heate of the other) can yeeld nothing else but the effects of an excessiue and immoderate colde cause lying in the veines, and mixed with the blood. Such are esteemed to bee dulnesse of conceit, blockishnesse, mopishnesse, and sottishnesse, one of the worst kindes of accidents that commonly ensue ouer-hardened, cooled and dryed melancholy in our bodies.

Againe, such as the partes of the blood be, such also is thought the blood to bee, and as the blood prooueth, so likewise are the spirites affected, for they doo issue and proceed from the blood it selfe.

And such as the spirites are, such also is adiudged to be the temper and dissipation of the heart and braine: and as the braine is disposed and affected, so likewise are the vertues of conceit, imagination, vnderstanding, and remembrance, affected and disposed also. All which in particular, by sundrie examples were easie to prooue, for him that is but meanely seene and slenderly read in Philosophie sayings, that the sanguine man by meanes of the puritie of his blood, hath his braine and inward parts well tempered, his sences cleare, his spirites light and subtile, his heart bold and merrie, his minde affable, curteous and ciuil. Whereas on the contrary part, the melancholy person by reason of the superfluous earthly and drie matter mixed with his bloud, hath his complexion more wan and swarte, his conceit of braine more dull and hard, his minde giuen to sollitarinesse and priuate life. For those two humours of bloud and melancholy, are in both their qualities very repugnant and contrary. The one being hotte and moyst, the other colde and drie.

But here me thinkes I hear you say, what maketh this idle discourse of bloud and melancholy, of the disposition of the braine and spirits to your purpose, or to the reputation of *Tabacco*?

Forsoothe very much. For heereby it appeareth that the continuall practises of *Tabacco*, destroy the puritie and clearnesse of their bloud, in that as I prooued before, it hardeneth and thickeneth the same. And in thickening it engendereth dull & mel-

A Warning for Tobacconists

ancholy spirites, which make blockish and sottish conceits, and a timerous and deiected mind not fit or conuenient for man that delilghteth in ciuilitie and societie of others. For seeing that the fewme of *Tabacco* yeeldeth no good foode or nourishment to the pure blood, but rather troubleth and corrupteth the same, it is thereby most plaine and euident, that it ingendreth in vs most dull and troubled spirites, also tasting and sauouring much of that loathsome fewme and duskish smoake which riseth & steemeth vp to the braine by the roofe and pallate of the mouth, first sent thither through the *Tabacco* pipe full charged with *Tabacco* dust, and afterward scorched and incinerated by the extreame heate of the parching fire.

This darke and smoakie fume, pearsing the cauities and ventricles of the braine, no otherwise, then a melancholy winde or adust vapour (rising from an adust Liuer, or obstructed splene) do breed in vs terror, and feare, discontentment of life, false and peruerse imaginations, and fantasies most strange, no way depending vpon iust cause or grounds, and alwaies a melancholy spirit, a fertfull and timerous minde. For truly the inward darknesse and obscuritie of the braine, doth appall and terrifie our inward sences and minde also, in no lesse sort then doth the externall darknesse or myst of the outward aire, terrifie & apall the same.

And if any man be farre blinded with *Tabacco*, that he will not admit for true, that the vapour or fume thereof ascending to the braine, is darke and

81

swart of colour, and of qualitie excessiue drie; let him but cast his eyes on the smoake issuing forth of the nosthrils of the *Tabacconists*, or to the smoakie tincture left in the *Tabacco* Pipe after the receit thereof, and he shall easily reclaime his error. This swart & sottish tincture cleaueth so fast to the inward part of the Pipe, as hardly by any means but by the extreme heate of the fire it may be cleared from thence. And no doubt the like impression doth the same leaue in our braines, and in the cauities thereof. So that the animall spirits ingendred in those places, can no lesse but (participating thereof) sauour of the same, no otherwise then wine put into an vnsauorie and mustie bottle, doth euer sauour of a mustie taste.

Neither am I any waies ignorant that *Aristotle* in his Problems holdeth that melancholy doth help and profit much to the sharpening & quickning of the wit and vnderstanding: and that melancholy persons are deemed of him the most wisest. But this kinde of melancholy (which *Aristotle* talketh of) is altogether naturall, and no way engendreth of the *Tabacco* smoake. For it is the sediment and groundes of the pure & perfect blood, in colour like golde, or somewhat inclining to purple: litle in quantitie, and somewhat shining. The spirits which issue from this kinde of melancholy, are verie light, fine and subtile, not much vnlike to the spirits of wine well distilled, and artificially rectified: which is by art and force of the fire drawne out of the feces or grounds of pure wine. And the spirits rising from this drie melancholy humor, are the thinner and the more subtile by reason of the closenesse & straightnesse of the pores of the same matter: and they are the more firme & constant in their action, by meanes that they issue and proceed from an humor more compacted and close vnited.

The subtilitie therefore and stabilitie of these spirites, rising from such a naturall melancholy, doeth much further the sharpning of the wit and vnderstanding of man.

But the like cannot be expected of the spirites rising of that kinde of melancholy which is engendred by the abuse of *Tabacco*. For this sort of melancholy humor is neither bright & shining like to molten gold, nor yet the grounds of pure and perfect blood, but rather an earthly and adust matter, not much vnlike stoncole or scorched earth. So that the spirites issuing from it must needs be of a diuers and farre contrarie qualitie and nature.

Last of all, melancholy being of nature cold and drie, had in reason need of some thin and liquid humor to be mixed therewith, to temper his extreame siccetie and drythe: which is the qualitie of most offence and annoyance in it. For as phlegme offendeth most in cold, so doth melancholy falt most in drynesse.

Tabacco therefore ought in no respect to be familiarly vsed of the melancholy person, because it is excessiue drie, both in his manifest qualitie, and likewise by accidentall meanes of his immoderate purging and euacuation, by meanes whereof, great part of that liquid and moyst matter is purged out of the body that should retaine and keepe it in perfect state and temper. And for that *Tabacco* is confessed to be hotte, almost in the third degree of excesse, therfore his drithe and siccetie is thereby made the more vehement, and vntollerable.

So that it is apparant that vnnaturall melancholy, whether it be made of adustian of bloud, choller, or phlegmy, or else of the sediment of them, scorched and as it were incinerated, hath no small encrease by the vntimely vse of this phantasticall deuice of *Tabacco* smoake, leauing in our bodies a fierie impression and drie distemper, not easily remedied.

And therefore in my opinion all melancholy persons, of what state or condition soeuer they bee of, and especially Students and Schollers, ought to bee very well aduised in the vse of so pernitious and dangerous a thing, least that in them, naturall melancholy be conuerted into vnnaturall, and this also, either into a corrisiue and adust humour apt to inflame the braine, or else into a matter so hard and drie, as that it be altogether hurtful and offensiue to the vnctuous and radicall moisture of the life of man: and thereby occasion a hastie and vntimely death. For no longer can life continue, then naturall heate bee refreshed with an ayrie and moderate moisture included in the radicall humour, and appointed by nature for the reliefe and sustentation of the same.

FINIS.

The
Womens Complaint
against Tobacco:

or,

An Excellent help to Multiplication.

Pespicuously Shewing the Annoyance that it
Brings to Mankind, and the Great Deprivation
of Comfort and Delight to the Female Sex, with
a Special and Significant Order Set Forth by the
VVomen for Suppressing the General use thereof
amongst their Husbands, they Finding that Tobacco is the Only Enemy to Pleasure and Procreation as they Now Plainly Make It Appear
in This Their Declaration.

(1675)

The
Womens Complaint
against Tobacco

A t a Sessions of Women lately holden at Gossips Hall; amongst the rest of their grievances which were then debated of, this great question arose, concerning the use of Tobacco: whether it was necessary that their Husbands should take Tobacco or no? a two minutes silence was made, (which was a great wonder) one more graver then the rest, begins to declare her self an utter Enemy to Tobacco, in this manner.

Neighbours and Friends, quoth she, I have been married to my Husband about fourteen years, this Man hath been all his time a great Smoaker, and to tell you the truth I was never got with child by him but once, and that was so feebly done, that I may boldly say it was not half gotten, though he is a Man as likely as any of his Neighbours, and as for my own part I am sure I am not in the least defective, but am as apt and fit for the work of generation as any of my Neighbours, nay I may say as likely to be got with child as any Woman in England, let the other be what she will, yet this Man cannot do the feat, and the reason why it is not done, I must clearly impute to his smoking that Infernal Indian Weed, which they call Tobacco, as for example. My next Neighbour Mrs. Twattle, her Husband and she have been married but nine years, and she has brought him nine brave lusty Children, well gotten Children, and the reason is, because her Husband never takes Tobacco; this I think may be a strong evidence that this filthy Weed is altogether destructive to procreation and robs a Woman of that sweet natural delight, which she ought to receive from her Husband or from some body else: Thus much I can testifie of my self, which I desire you would take into consideration, and proceed to further Judgement according to your best knowledge.

This witty Oration so tickled the fancy and imagination of the rest of this Female Assembly, that they could scarce forbear speaking all at once, but silence was again commanded, but could not be obtained for a good while, at length a handsome, comely, buxome Woman stands up, and desires to be heard, and passes her sentence thus. Tobacco! O cursed Tobacco? I wish that Man had been hang'd that first brought thee over into England; for I have a pritty young Man to my Husband, as you all know Neighbours; and by his countenance appears to be a good Womans Man, but I am sure 'tis I that find the contrary, I am sure I have heard my Grandmother say, (but indeed she was old) that one Man was enough for one Woman) but (O this damn'd Tobacco) I am sure I find it nothing so, for I could dispence with two or three such Men as my Husband; Alas, what is once in three Weeks? or once a Month for a young brisk Woman who could willingly enjoy a Man every night; to be sure; if not a little in the day time? Well, if this be the effects of Tobacco, I am resolv'd my Husband shall leave it off, or Ile leave him off, and betake my self to some other Man, that shall take no Tobacco, but shall refresh himself and me, sometimes at the Tavern with good brisk Wine, and a good Dinner or Supper, and sometimes carry me to see a Play, and sometimes cross the water to Spring-Garden, and there eat and drink well; and when the Night comes he shall wait on me home to my Chamber, and there briskly to supply the wants of a longing Woman, as it may be my self; all this I will have instead of Tobacco, or else Ile want of my will; who can endure to have a smoaky Chimny lye by her all night nay more then all this, the stinking Brute must kiss you, thinking to satisfie you with that; for alas he can do nothing else: For there is no Oyl left in the Lamp, that is all wasted and consumed by

smoaking, and fuming that stinking unnatural, destructive Devil, Tobacco: O how I am transported
with hatred and aversion towards this Weed, when
I call to mind how destructive it is to the pretious
Nature of Man, which was made for the supply of
us Women; and not to be spung'd up by Tobacco,
whose Original sprung from Hell, for the Devil
(who thinks he never ensnares men fast enough)
invented this stinking dry Weed, that Men taking
of it their mouths will so stink, and their throats be
so parched & scorched with the heat thereof, that
they must drink excessively to quench the inflama-
tion thereof, till at length they become drunk; then
are they fit for all manner of debauchery, which is
the ready road to destruction. How say you Neighbours have not I spoke divinely, I am confident that
there is ne're a Woman here, but will willingly set
her Seal to the truth of these Objections, which I
have here experimentally declared before this worthy Assembly. And if it comes to my turn to speak
again I can yet say more on this subject, which may
be as much significant to the good and benefit of
our Sex as what I have already spoken.

She having thus spoken they signified their as-
sention by a general applause of what she had declared: but still striving who should be next; there
was a great and terrible combustion amongst
themselves: till at length a Doctors Wife claimed
the preheminence; saying, that she (from the experience she had learned from her Husbands books)
could discover and lay open unto them, the many

and injurious impediments that were occasioned in the body of Man by the poysonous fume of the Tobacco: and how obnoxious it is to the Seminal; and luxurious parts of those Men, that take delight in sucking in the venome of that dull Leaf.

The rest hearing her begin thus learnedly were resolved to be silent a while, and bridle their tongues, expecting that she would unfold some secret evil that lay lurking in this broad Leaf of Tobacco: So she begun her discourse after this skilful method.

Neighbours (quoth she) it has been my fortune to have been twice marryed; Yet I must also let you know, that I am still but young in years, not surpassing the age of thirty: I was marryed to my first Husband but three years, and then he dyed; and in that time I had no child by him; nor half that satisfaction from him, which a young Woman (as I was) might expect: but I knew no better then; though I have had a large and comfortable experience since I buryed him, and married the Doctor; who is now my Husband by whom I have had six Children, and all the delights which are due to the Marriage bed. I once took an occasion to ask him what he thought might be the reason that I had no Children by my former Husband, who in his life time appeared to be a likelyer Man then himself: he made me this Answer, that he took too much Tobacco: For (saith he) Tobacco is of it self hot and dry, and destroys the Radical Moisture; Now I hope you know what is meant by the Radical Moisture, for it is the seed in Man which propagates and begets Children in women; Now that being wanting, those Men are altogether unfit for procreation; and this vacancy of Nature is occasioned by Mens smoaking that base destructive Weed called Tobacco: Nay a further account I can yet give you of it's operations; for reading lately in one of my Husbands books I found it thus written, first in Latine;

Destrnctio generis humani Nicotiana: Semen radicale exaruit, Pericranio venenum infundit; Sic vita humana perfecta. This I did not understand, but reading on I found it thus Englished. The Weed Tobacco is the destruction of humane Race, for it dryes up the Radical Moisture, and throws such poysonous vapours into the Brain, that it sends many untimely unto their Graves.

This being heard they began to be weary of silence every one striving who should give this Doctress the greatest applause: but she desired them to forbear, for she had not finisht her discourse; so then they again seated themselves as before. Now, says she, which of you all will suffer your Husbands or Bedfellows, to take this cursed Tobacco that fills their heads full of inflamations, conflagrations, proclamations, incendiaries, combustions, and such like hard words, which sends them to their graves in the prime of their age; Nay moreover it robs & deprives us women of that consolation & delight which every young woman ought to enjoy in a full measure.

I say it steals away all those happinesses from us, even whilst our Husbands are alive with us, and at last tumbles them over the perch as they call it, by consumption Coughs, and such like languishing distemper.

At that they all unanimously cryed out away with this cursed Tobacco, this venemous Indian Weed, we do clearly vote it down to be a common and publick Enemy to Men, in robbing of them of their health and strength but a private and secret Enemy to Women in robbing them of their pleasure and Delight. Silence again was order'd by the grand Matron of the Assembly, who to tell you the truth was well striken in years, and yet she would very fain have had her vote amongst the rest, but she was very gently and mildly prohibited by the younger sort they very fairly alledging that there was enough of them to mannage this cause, whose warmer blood runs briskly through their veins, and truly it dos altogether belong to us, for Tobacco could in no wise be injurious to her, whom Time already had deprived of the enjoyments of mankind, but the harm it did was to those who were capable of receiving the benefits of Nature, but were made destitute thereof by reason of their sottish Husbands, who make Chimneys of their throats and change their Teeth from their natural colour to be as black as the Chimney stock; 'tis we I say, that have just cause to make our timely and most just complaint against this surfeiting, unnaturall stinking Weed, least in a few years we find a dissolution of mankind, and then I am sure the World will soon be at an end, for we Women be we never so active, cannot pleasure one another in that great work of generation, neither can we Multiply: Poor Souls we shall be starved unless a speedy course be taken for the extirpation and rooting up of this great and destructive enemy to our mournful Sex.

The old Gentlewoman hearing these great reasons, did willingly give place to the younger Dames, confessing the truth, that her dancing days were done, and she cared no more for Man, then Man cared for her, but yet Girls quoth she, I have a fellow feeling of your sad and languishing conditions; Well, well my pretty Rogues stand up for your privilledges, I was young once and could as ill dispence with a defective Man, as the briskest Dame in town, though I say it my self, and truly my pretty Lambs, I must advise you to make the best use of your time, and take away those things, and causes, which in any wise do obstruct or hinder your delight and pleasure in this World: For truly, old age will quickly come. Time to my knowledge hath Wings, and flies away with a swift pace, O methinks it is but yesterday since I embraced a pretty young Man a friend of mine, when as alas it is now above twenty years since, yet I cannot forget the sweet delight and pleasure I then receiv'd: In my Conscience Girls, if I should talk of it a little longer, old bal'd pated Time would retreat, and I should become young again; but O alas the Chollick now doth gripe me, the Cramp doth draw my Limbs together sorely, Diseases encompass me round about, and I must give way to younger heads to manage this great work of Women-kind, and when the Bill is pass'd for the voting down of this filthy Tobacco, if I cannot put my hand to it, to shew my willingness and my well wishings to our Sex, I will put one finger to it, and thus I will take my leave of you, finding my self something faint, in speaking what I have said already, Ah this old Age, I say it cannot be hid, be sure you vigorously proceed against this cursed Tobacco, that is your open enemy, and so farewell.

With that they all gave her many and hearty thanks, for her good counsel and advise, either of them being more sensible of the great injuries it did their Husbands (and so consequently themselves) then she was, by reason old Age had not yet overtaken them.

Now again, it was to be considered who should speak next, all of them still having something to say and declare, though much to the same effect which had been said already; till at length a nimble tongued Lass, desired that her verdict might be heard, not doubting (as she told them) that what she had to offer and propose, might be as significant and effectual to the business in hand, as any thing that had been said and declared by any of them: for truly she had the sence of fellow feeling upon her as much as the best of them, though as yet not actually known the pleasures of Man: for (saith she) I am now upwards of seventeen, and by your selves you may know that a Woman in my condition has a longing desire to be further satisfied concerning the enjoyment of mankind.

They hearing her so violently urge upon this point, gave order that she should be heard with great attention and diligence, not knowing but her aggrievances might equally compare with their own, so they commanded her to speak as boldly as her Sex and tender years would admit and allow of: so she declared her self briefly after this manner. Neighbours (quoth she) I understand that the drift of our present business is to disanul and make void this Weed Tobacco, and to prohibit and forbid all mankind in general as well Batchelors as married Men, from taking or smoaking any more of it, from this time forward, and for evermore.

Now the reasons that I shall infer upon my own account (for I suppose you will expect that I should nominate some principal grounds) shall be these. I being as yet a Virgin (though it may be contrary to my own will shall be afraid to marry, fearing I should marry and tye my self to a Man that should take Tobacco, and that I thereby should be deprived of those enjoyments and delight which every Woman expects after Marriage: For you do all agree with me that Tobacco is the great Thief that robs all our Sex of their natural pleasures: The apprehension and fear of this Tobacco for ought I know, may be the utter ruine and destruction, not only of my self, but of many thousand Damsels more, for it may cause them never to marry, expecting no comfort nor consolation from a smoak-

er: so that they will be forced to live and dye Maids
as they call us, then shall we be forced, as our great
Grandmothers have left upon record, to lead Apes
in Purgatory; the sence of which torment I think
is sufficient to disswade all Men from taking Tobacco, if they have any tenderness of hearts towards us, and to perswade you the Governours of
this honourable Assembly to enact something so
strong, that all Men may be afraid hence-forward
to smoak any more of that stinking weed: and that
I leave to your wiser breasts to go forward with;
for you have been (as you have declared) sufficient
sufferers by your Husbands smoaking this fuming and suffocating Indian Leaf. She having thus
ended they gave a general consent to what she had
said to be very significant; and now they proceed
to make an order order for the prohibition of their
Husbands taking Tobacco, and thus they begun.

Imprimis, We do declare that our Will and
Pleasure is, that no Man whatsoever, Married or
unmarryed, under the Age of fifty years old, (then
started up a young woman and said, pray let it be
sixty) No, no, said she hold your peace, I say no Man
under the Age of fifty years old, shall at any time,
or upon any occasion whatsoever, take, smoak,
or draw into his Mouth the smoak of that cursed
stinking Weed called Tobacco, for the grounds and
Reasons above-mentioned, which are sufficiently
known to our selves. Now if any Man shall at any
time he perverse, and will not obey these our or-
ders; then it shall be lawful for the Wife of such a

man, to choose, and take unto her self, a Friend, or Gallant, such a man as shall seem most pleasant in her Eyes: this we do license and permit in case of the like default.

FINIS.

Index

A

Aeneid (Virgil) 72
Aethiopia 73
agues 19, 50
Alexander Severus 23
Aloes Socotrina 66
Ambrose of Milan 36, 54
Apollo 38
Arabians 67
Aristotle 35, 36, 49, 53, 82
arteries 63
Attienagoras Argivus 73
Augustine of Hippo 36
Avicenna 63, 71

B

Barwick 29
Bath 57
blood 77, 78, 80, 84
bones 63
brain 6, 12, 13, 19, 21, 26, 33,
    36, 37, 39, 52, 54, 55, 67,
    80, 81, 84

C

Calabria 67
Camarinds 67
cannibals 38
Cassellius 36
Cassia 67
catarrh 63

cholics 14
Christians 42, 75, 76
Clusius, Carolus 34
Comment vpon Garcaeas de Stirpibus et Aromaticis Indicis (Clusius) 34
coughs 63

D

Devil, the 75, 76
dropsy 45
drunkards 17, 21

E

East Indies 72
effeminacy 23
England 19, 28, 29, 38, 39, 43, 68, 88, 89
Englishmen 73

F

fellowship 24
flatulence 14
flesh 63
France 8

G

Galen of Pergamon 35, 44, 63, 64, 65, 71, 72, 76, 77, 78
Galenus, Aelius. *See* Galen of Pergamon
Gellius, Aulus 71
gipsum plaster 68
gout 19
Guyana 38

H

henbane 67
heretics 38
Hilarion 36
Hippocrates 35, 58, 66

I

Indians 8, 9, 19, 23, 31, 34, 37, 38, 44, 66, 70, 72, 73, 75, 88, 93, 97
Israel 21
Italy 71

J

Jerome of Stridon 36
Jews 22

K

kidneys 14
kidney stones 14

L

Laelius, Gaius 36
lethargy 20
ligaments 63
liver 11

M

Manna 67
mariners 73, 74
Marsitians 71, 72
medicine 20
melancholy 76, 77, 78, 79, 80, 81, 82, 83, 84
Monardes, Nicolás Bautista 34, 48, 71, 75, 76

N

nose 13, 14, 25

O

opium 65, 67, 72, 73

P

Parve, Ambrose 54
Persian Empire 22
philosophers 24, 53, 61
phlegm 77, 83
physicians 4, 5, 9, 16, 17, 18, 34, 35, 42, 47, 50, 51, 52, 55, 58, 66
Plato 35, 36, 53
Pliny the Elder 71
Pluto 39, 61
poison 10, 65, 69, 71, 72, 73, 74
Poorhouses 22
Porta, Giambattista della / Giovanni Battista della 34
priests 19, 42, 75
Puritans 19

R

rheumes 42, 63
Rhubarbe 67
Roman Empire 22
Rome 72

S

scorpions 73
scourings 63
scurvy 73
Segunda parte del libro des las cosas que se traen de nues-
tras Indias Occidentales (Monardes) 75
Seneca 69
Sextus Empericus 73
Siluius Italicus 71
sinews 63
slaves 9, 19
Spain 38
Spaniards 8, 9
spatterings 63
spleen 81
stomach 11, 14, 19, 20, 44, 48, 55, 56, 68
Sulpitius Severus 36

T

temperamentis, De (Galen) 63
Tobias son of Tobit 19
Turkey 9
Turks 72
Twattle, Mrs 88

U

universities 15
urine 14

V

Varro, Marcus Terentius 36
veins 63
vipers 69, 71, 72
Virgil 72
viribus cordis, De (Avicenna) 71
vomit 51, 56, 57, 63, 67

W

Wales 29, 30

wine 21, 50, 89
worms 70